MASTER YOUR EMOTIONS

MASTER
YOUR EMOTIONS

VIRGINIA LLOYD

FREEDOM PUBLICATIONS

Freedom Publications
P.O. Box 32095
Phoenix, Arizona 85064

Library of Congress Catalog Card
Number: 85-82067

ISBN 0-915721-01-5

First printing 1986

Book Design
T.R. Carbonel
T.R. & Associates, Inc.
Glendale, AZ

TABLE OF CONTENTS

PREFACE

The intention of this book is to provide information about emotions, which I hope will inspire greater insight into your own personal emotional nature. This information was developed in over ten years of leading Sedona Institute seminars, which present a specific technique to let go of stressful feelings. This material is still a major part of the Sedona Institute Basic Course.

While there are exercises included which I believe will allow you to begin mastering your emotions, the book is not intended to replace anything you're already doing that you feel is constructive and helpful for you. Additionally, it is not meant to be a substitute for seeking competent professional help if you should decide that you need it.

No book can take the place of your attendance at a good seminar, or personal contact with a resource you find helpful, such as a minister, priest, rabbi or therapist (if those are things you want to do). However, I truly believe this book can be a wonderful supplement to any discipline, therapy or counseling.

After you've read it, you can continue to refer to it as your own personal guidebook. You may want to read again the chapters that are most interesting to you or try some of the suggested ways of helping yourself out of negative feelings. Allow yourself to start enjoying your life. I believe that once you begin to understand your feelings, you'll see that you don't have to be the victim of them anymore—and that can make all the difference.

I hope you enjoy the book and more importantly, I hope you find it helpful.

ACKNOWLEDGEMENTS

I'd like to thank the following people who, knowingly or unknowingly, were instrumental in making this book happen.

First, to all of you who take the courses we teach at Sedona Institute, I thank you from my heart. Your courage and willingness to look at your feelings and let them go is always an inspiration to me.

To our Sedona Institute staff, a group of dedicated individuals who give generously of themselves to help bring the Releasing^{SM} technique to all those who want it: Ernest Castaldo, Annrika James, Janet Bechtel, Jan Stoltman, Ginger Haney, Del Haney, Rick Solomon, Keith Varnum, Kate Freeman, Jim Hurley, Jeanne Fitzsimmons and Hale Dwoskin.

A very special thanks to Annrika James, who gave so generously of her talent, advice, encouragement and time. She also did the illustration on page 8.

To Rick Handel and his staff, Noel Foronda, Maria Francisco, Patrick Kernan, Ron Bucalo and Scott Gibbs.

To Jan Stoltman for her generous and helpful editorial comments and suggestions.

To Mary Hawkins for her gentle editing.

To Tom Carbonel for his knowledge, patience, professionalism, and good humor.

To Sally Jessy Raphael, Dr. Shelley Uram and Dr. Lou Ormont for reading the manuscript and liking it enough to write a cover comment.

To Larry Crane for his enthusiasm.

To Hal Landers for his invaluable advice and expertise.

To Dr. Tessa Albert Warschaw for her support and encouragement.

To the memory of my father, who lived courageously and always encouraged me to be myself and do my best.

To my mother, who greets life with love and a terrific sense of humor.

To my sons, Richard and Eric, who have enriched my life in many ways.

To Lester, whose influence is on every page. If it weren't for him, this book could not have been written.

And finally to myself, for "hanging in there."

"I want you to discover, through your own experience, the unlimited, terrific and perfect being you are! I want you to have, be, and do whatever you will or desire." *

Lester Levenson
Founder of the Sedona Institute

*From the book *Choose Freedom* by Virginia Lloyd.

PART ONE

WHAT ARE YOU FEELING RIGHT NOW?

Emotions! It seems that you're never without them. Oh, sometimes they're quiet, not particularly bothering you, but somehow you know they're there, lurking in the background, just waiting for something to happen. And when it does, WHAM! You feel mad, you feel sad, you feel bad, and you just don't know what to do.

All of your thoughts, attitudes and feelings are colored by your emotions. The job or career you have, the kind of person you marry, how you get along with people, every area of your life is influenced by your emotions. In fact, your success or failure in life is actually determined by how well you're able to deal with your negative feelings. Unfortunately, most people try to ignore their negative feelings, rather than deal with them, because they don't quite know how to handle them.

Often, you'll try to *suppress* the feelings...push them down into the subconscious so you can forget that you have them.

If that doesn't work and you're still reeling under the attack, you might try the *escape* route...drugs, alcohol, sex, quit the job, leave the person, move to another town. Or you might try to talk yourself into feeling better.

But sometimes you can't do those things, so, the only thing left is to *express* the feelings...cry your eyes out, shout at people, punch them in the nose. Right?

Wrong! You can *get rid* of your negative emotions, and the best part is that it can be easy—and it's fun. The first step is to get a good look at your negative emotions, rather than hiding your head in the sand.

It's important to realize that you are unique. The decisions you've made about the way the world is and how you should behave in it evolved through your own special combination of birth, upbringing, circumstances of life and, most importantly, your reaction to things you've been told. In brief, your belief system.

However, the things you were told may not have been correct, and decisions you made when you were a child do not often serve you well as an adult. In addition, they result in a lot of misunderstanding, guilt and pain, and prevent your natural beauty from shining through. So it's important to become aware of the negative elements which are no longer helpful, and get rid of them.

This book is written to fill that basic need. It presents emotions in a clear, easy to understand sequence and walks you through each one. At the end of each segment, there are suggested remedies to help you when you get stuck. There's also some space for you to add your own remedies and thoughts about each emotion.

By reading and following the simple steps outlined in this book, you will achieve the following:

1) You will have a more complete understanding of your own emotional makeup.

2) You will be able to better understand your friends, loved ones and other people.

3) You will have explored the concept that it is possible to get rid of unwanted feelings, and what that can mean to you.

4) You'll have come to know your new best friend (you!) a lot better.

First, let's look at some information about the mind which will help you to understand your negative emotions and how to overcome them.*

---

*This material is from the Sedona Method℠ Basic Course, which teaches a way to let go of uncomfortable and destructive emotions.

CHAPTER 1

OUR MINDS
ARE LIKE COMPUTERS

In order to understand your emotional makeup, it is important to have a picture of the mind and how it works. It's not difficult to understand if you're open and willing to suspend some of your preconceived ideas.

We all have programs in our minds. These are thoughts, ideas, decisions and conclusions about the world, other people and ourselves. Just as a computer is programmed, we program these thoughts and ideas into our minds where we hold them for future reference.

The place where these thoughts and ideas are stored we call the subconscious part of the mind. If you consider the prefix "sub," you'll note that it means "below," i.e., subterranean means below the earth; subway means below the way or road; and submarine means below the water. Therefore, when I use the word "subconscious," I mean below the level of conscious awareness. It's the part of the mind we're not aware of. We store our programs in the subconscious, like a computer, so that our conscious thoughts can be directed to the everyday business at hand. These programs in the subconscious work automatically, often to our own detriment.

Even though we are not consciously aware of its workings, our mind functions like a computer. Programs are stored in the subconscious until events in our world cause them to be recalled. Then those programs override anything else that may be going on at the time.

For example, a program "people cannot be trusted," might cause you to disbelieve a declaration from someone who honestly loves you, even though that person might have an outstanding reputation for honesty and integrity. You might even start to question that person's motives, when the fact is that he or she truly loves you and just wants to do things for you. That not uncommon type of negative programming colors your entire world, and your perception of everything around you.

Understanding the mind is the first step to conquering it and regaining control of it.

The mind is really very simple. It just appears to be complicated because of our subconscious programs, which continually influence our thinking, our feelings and our behavior.

THERE ARE BASICALLY THREE ASPECTS TO THE MIND.

The First Aspect Of Mind:
Your Sense Of Identity

The First Aspect of the mind which will help you to understand your emotional makeup and put you in control is the sense of identity, the "I" sense. This could be described as "My sense of who I am."

The "I" alone has no limits. When the "I" identifies with a personality, it moves into the realm of mind; the "I" becomes the ego and assumes limitations. "I" becomes "I, Virginia," or "I, Rick," or "I, James."

So we could say that your "I" sense is your unlimited, all powerful Beingness, now identified with and confined to a limiting identity.

INFINITE, UNLIMITED, ALL-ENCOMPASSING	"I" becomes	Mary, with all of Mary's limitations

The Second Aspect Of Mind:
Your Ability To Discriminate

The Second Aspect of the mind which will help you understand your emotional makeup and begin to see how you can deal with your negative emotions is the Discriminator, and that represents your ability to discriminate.

Discrimination — The ability to perceive things correctly as they are.

From time to time, we've all experienced a lack of discrimination. Here are some examples of that lack of discrimination on the physical level:

You put soured cream in your coffee, but because you're upset and your mind is on something else, you drink most of it before you notice that it's curdled and tastes bad.

A friend says that he'll meet you at 5 o'clock but because you want to meet him at 3 o'clock, *you think* he said he'd be there at 3. Then when he arrives at 5, you're furious with him.

You buy a new black skirt, only to find out later that it's really navy blue in color.

Lack of discrimination operates the same way on an abstract or emotional level:

You think a friend is angry with you, when she's not.

You think people don't like you, when they do.

You think you've done something wrong, when you haven't.

You've done something wrong and you think it's right.

You think your boss is going to fire you; instead, you receive congratulations for a good job.

Discrimination is the ability to tell one thing from another.

For example, if you perceive that you're holding a *book* in your *hand*, you have just discriminated. You perceived correctly that your hand and the book are two different things. You did not believe that your hand and the book were one and the same.

When people totally lose their ability to discriminate, they cannot tell one thing from another. They might look at a cup of coffee and believe it to be a vase of flowers. They might even start smelling the flowers which are not there. They lose their sense of reality.

As you can see, the ability to discriminate is extremely important for your emotional well-being. I'll go even further and say that it is the key to having clarity and peace of mind.

Discrimination is the key to understanding your negative feelings, and to getting rid of them.

The Third Aspect Of Mind:
Sensing, Recording, Replaying

This brings us to The Third Aspect of the mind which will help you understand your emotional makeup and how the subconscious programs were developed. We could call it the "Programs Aspect" because it represents the way in which information is obtained and stored in our subconscious programs. This is the computer section of the mind.

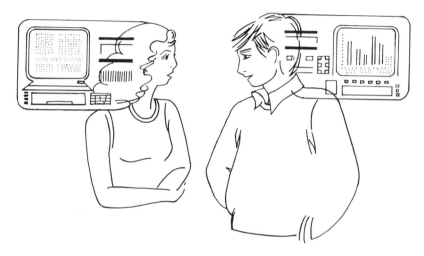

Often, it's more like programs talking to each other than people communicating.

The Senses

This is also the section which provides the "I" sense with a link with the world through the physical senses of sight, hearing, taste, touch and smell.

Your physical senses act as sensors, relaying information back to your "I" sense about your environment. Then you make decisions as to your actions based on that information.

For example:

If your *heat sensor* tells you the room temperature has dropped, you can get a sweater to wear;

If your *smelling* sense tells you your cake is burning, you can turn off the oven;

If your *visual* sense tells you it's raining outside, you can close the windows;

If your *taste* sense tells you the food is spoiled, you can throw it away;

If your *hearing* sense tells you someone just rang the doorbell, you can go to the door.

In other words, your actions are determined by two things:

a) what your senses convey to your "I" sense and

b) what you then decide is appropriate to do in the situation.

THE THREE ASPECTS OF MIND

	Aspect 1	Aspect 2	Aspect 3
The Aspect	The "I" Sense	The Discriminator	Sensing Recording Replaying
What it is	My Sense of Who I Am	My Ability to Discriminate	My Programs Aspect
How the Three Aspects Interact	"I" $\rightarrow$	through my discriminator $\rightarrow$	receive messages from my senses telling me what's going on in my world.
The Result	THEN BASED ON THE INFORMATION RECEIVED, I MAKE DECISIONS ABOUT MY ACTIONS.		

Thus, *based on what you perceive,* you make decisions as to your behavior. Your decisions can be appropriate only as long as messages from the senses come through freely and are not distorted in any way. Your senses and your discriminator must both be fully and freely operating.

The problem is that we may rarely receive a totally undistorted message. There is too much static in our receivers, and our discriminators are never fully open!

The importance of keeping the discriminator open as much as possible becomes apparent. We also begin to see the importance of knowing what closes it, and this relates to our negative emotions, or what we at the Sedona Institute call "AGFLAP.™"

QUESTION: What is AGFLAP?

ANSWER: AGFLAP represents the negative emotional states. It stands for:

Apathy—lowest energy level. Apathy is the "lack of feeling or emotion; impassiveness; lack of interest or concern; indifference."

Grief—next lowest energy level. Grief is the "intense emotional suffering caused by loss, misfortune, injury or evils of any kind; sorrow; regret."

Fear—a chaotic energy level. Fear is a "feeling of anxiety and agitation caused by the presence or nearness of danger, evil, pain, etc.; timidity; dread; apprehension."

Lust—the energy level that gets us moving. Lust is an "overmastering desire; eagerness to possess or enjoy; a desire to gratify the senses; bodily appetite."

Anger—intense and destructive energy level. Anger is "a strong feeling excited by a real or supposed injury; often accompanied by a desire to take vengeance, or to obtain satisfaction from the offending party; resentment; wrath; ire."

Pride—a holding energy level. Pride is "an overhigh opinion of oneself; exaggerated self-esteem; conceit."

QUESTION: What causes the discriminator to close?

ANSWER: Many elements can cause the discriminator to close. Among these are: drugs, alcohol, bright lights, loud noises, repetition, conflicting messages, pain, illness, threats, violence, confusion, pressure.

However, the most important element that closes the discriminator is our feelings, our emotions. This is because we have them with us all the time.

Also, we might feel we have a little control over some of the other elements which affect us, but not over our feelings. For instance, we can often get away from the loud noise, we can abstain from drugs and alcohol, we can leave the pressure situation. But we don't believe that we can get away from our feelings.

QUESTION: What are feelings?

ANSWER: Feelings are the devices used by your internal computer to provoke you into an automated response. They spring from the way you have been programmed.

QUESTION: If feelings spring from the programs, then wouldn't it be logical to say that it is actually the programs that close the discriminator?

ANSWER: Yes. On a deeper level these subconsciously held, previously decided upon, programs of how the world is and how we should behave in it do in fact close the discriminator. That's because these preconceived concepts are ideas that prevent us from seeing things as they really are.

However, for our purposes, it's better to talk about feelings rather than programs, because it's easier to become aware of and discriminate on our feelings. And as you'll see, your ability to discriminate is the key to becoming free of unwanted negative feelings.

More About Your Mind And Its Programs

In the third aspect of mind, the programs aspect, the senses are the conscious manifestation of that aspect. This refers to our five physical senses which we are usually aware of even though we don't always think about them very much. This also refers to our feeling sense, which includes our emotions.

Your Automatic Pilot

The subconscious is designed as an automatic pilot. It was originally intended to provide for the autonomic body processes such as heartbeat, respiration, digestion, elimination, and so forth. This was to ensure that, in the unhappy event that a rock should fall on your head and render you unconscious, your heart would continue beating. Every normal baby is born with this automatic pilot already programmed and intact.

From day one, we are bombarded with information about our world, our environment. It is too much of a task to consciously process each item as it is presented, and a newborn baby has nothing with which to compare the information anyway. There is no way for it to determine whether a particular bit of information is accurate or not. So the infant just accepts it all as correct, and programs it, part and parcel, into the subconscious.

This goes on for the first several years of life. The child gets continual input from family members, primarily mother, father and siblings, as well as any others living in the home. Those early years are extremely important because information programmed at that time becomes the basis for evaluating all other information we receive as we go through life.

For example, people who are often called stupid as children have an almost insurmountable program which prevents them from recognizing their real intelligence. Even high marks and awards don't change that programmed sense of "I'm really stupid." And they often feel that the awards they've received are flukes and undeserved. Their thoughts might be, "If they really knew the truth about me, they'd take this award back." The fact that they are really brilliant might never occur to them because of their previous programming.

This illustrates an important fact: Objective reality makes no difference to the subconscious computer. The subconscious computer cannot discriminate, it can only respond in accordance with what has been programmed into it.

How The Subconscious Mechanism Works

The mechanism works through the feelings. For example, you probably have a program that says, "In order to keep this body machine going, I must refuel it three times a day."

What happens three times a day?

You feel hungry!

What does that feeling of hunger do?

It produces conscious thoughts about how to get food (fuel)!

The preprogrammed directive to refuel closes the discriminator and puts the individual on automatic in a quest for food.

Have you ever heard someone say, "I'm too hungry to think right now." In other words, his discriminator has closed to what's happening in the present, and the individual is following a direction to refuel, from the program stored in his subconscious.

Programs are from the past. A feeling is the manifestation in the present of an old program.

The mechanism works in exactly the same way when you're involved in an emotional feeling. An old program becomes activated and produces a feeling, which closes the

13

discriminator. Then the automatic pilot takes over, and directs the person's actions in accordance with that old program. In other words, the person's behavior is being directed by an old decision from the past, rather than by the "I" sense in the present.

The old program actually shuts down the discriminator and puts the individual on automatic—carrying out the pre-programmed directive from the past—and it accomplishes this through the feelings.

There are some important reminders to mention here:

1) a) The program-replay mechanism is designed to work when you're unconscious, i.e., if you should become unconscious or fall asleep, for example, your heart will continue to beat.

   b) Since it was designed that way, the mechanism actually works best when you're unconscious.

   c) Therefore, the mechanism will cause you to lose consciousness, if necessary, in order to carry out your previous instructions. For example, if a program to "get out of here" is strong enough, it could even cause you to faint if there were no other way to accomplish an escape. Usually, however, it is not that extreme and results only in a diminished awareness or lack of discrimination.

2) The purpose of the subconscious program/replay mechanism is to free the conscious mind to think of other things. Therefore, once you've programmed something into the subconscious, you can forget it.

3) With regard to the effectiveness of any particular program, there are four elements to consider.

   a) **Repetition** — The more occasions you have to reinforce the original program, the more powerful it becomes. Repetition plays an important part in programming.

b) **Force** — The force with which an instruction is given affects the overall power of the program.

c) **Physical State**—Another factor is our physical state at the time the program is put in. If we're ill or in pain, we're more vulnerable to being programmed.

d) **Emotional State** — Another very important factor is our emotional state at the time. This one is very important because it's an old program which is causing the emotional state to begin with. Therefore, any new instructions latch onto that old program and reinforce it. It also gives additional power to the new instructions because it will have all the power of the old program behind it.

4) Because the programs are from the past, we rarely understand why our feelings are the way they are in the present.

Outsmarting Your Programs

It starts to become obvious that a permanent solution to our problems does *not* lie in looking away from our negative feelings/programs and simply putting positive programs into our subconscious computer. As you can see from the above, the more programs we have, the less we can discriminate.

And it is important to realize that it makes no difference whether the programs are positive or negative. Any program, even a positive one, produces an automatic response and reduces your capacity to discriminate, to see things as they are.

The best way to achieve greater happiness and freedom is to *increase your capacity to discriminate.* This can be done by getting rid of the negative subconscious programs, the AGFLAP.

What is the advantage to letting go of the subconscious programs?

As you eliminate negative programs from the subconscious, your capacity to discriminate becomes more and more available to you. This naturally allows you to eliminate more and more of the programs and consequently gives you control over how your AGFLAP affects you, rather than your AGFLAP maintaining control over you, as it now does.

It allows you to be free to operate your life at the conscious level, where you are in control.

CHAPTER 2

EMOTIONS AS ENERGY LEVELS

Emotions are groups of feelings related to each other on the basis of energy. Each emotional state has two energy components—

1) **Holding Energy:** the amount of energy assigned to the programs and feelings (some of this energy is used to keep the programs suppressed); and

2) **Available Energy:** the amount of energy remaining and available for our use.

For example, if 90% of your total energy were assigned to your AGFLAP, you would only have 10% of your total energy available to use in productive activities.

Also, if 90% of your energy is assigned to your feelings, then your feelings have that amount of energy to use to control you, and you only have 10% remaining to combat them. Is it any wonder that the feelings are often the winners, and push you into behavior which can be harmful and destructive to yourself and others?

However, with awareness and discrimination, we can sometimes offset the control our feelings have over us. Once we're able to discriminate, the 10% of energy available to us can be used more efficiently. With increased awareness and clarity of focus, that 10% becomes like a laser beam to get rid of the negative feelings. This frees up more of our energy for productive use. The "remedies" section of each emotion suggests ways you can summon your energy resources to overcome the influence of your negative feelings, your AGFLAP.

Basically, emotions represent different energy levels. We *unconsciously* use these emotions to achieve various objectives or goals. Some examples of how we use the AGFLAP in this way are: We might cry to get a person to give us what we want. If that doesn't work, we might move up to another energy level and get angry to get what we want. Or we might use an emotion such as guilt in order to gain forgiveness or love if we feel that the other person disapproves of something we've done.

Becoming aware of how this works and gaining insight into the nature of feelings and emotions can free you from much of their hold over you. For example, if someone is shouting at you...and you're able to realize that the person is just trying to accomplish something with that feeling... you might be able to see a better way to deal with the situation than by getting yourself all worked up also. Rather than getting upset, you might decide to leave him or her alone to cool off. Or you might decide to let the person blow off steam for a while and let the whole thing blow over much more quickly. There are often options for our behavior which we can't see when feelings are in the way.

ENERGY SCALE OF EMOTIONS

EMOTION	ENERGY USED TO SUPPRESS	ENERGY AVAILABLE FOR ACTION

THE NEGATIVES—AGFLAP

EMOTION	ENERGY USED TO SUPPRESS	ENERGY AVAILABLE FOR ACTION
Apathy	100-95%	0- 5%
Grief	94-90%	5- 10%
Fear	89-85%	11- 15%
Lust	84-80%	16- 20%
Anger	79-70%	21- 30%
Pride	69-60%	31- 40%

THE POSITIVES—CAP

EMOTION	ENERGY USED TO SUPPRESS	ENERGY AVAILABLE FOR ACTION
Courageousness	59-35%	41- 65%
Acceptance	34-15%	66- 85%
Peace	14- 0%	86-100%

The above scale illustrates how our natural, inherent energy is diverted into the task of suppressing, and keeping suppressed, the feelings (past decisions—past programs).

Our mind, the computer, in turn, uses that energy to direct us into the thinking and patterns of behavior which have been predetermined by those past decisions or programs.

Now that you see how your mind works and how the emotions affect your energy, let's move on to the negative emotions, AGFLAP. Taking them one by one, you'll see how each emotion affects your ability to discriminate; how it takes control over your "I" sense; and how you can help your "I" sense to start taking charge again. It's an exciting journey.

"The chief cause of human error is to be found in prejudices picked up in childhood.

"The principal effect of the passions is that they incite and persuade the mind to will the event for which they prepared the body."

Rene Descartes (1596-1650)
French Philosopher

PART TWO

THE NEGATIVE EMOTIONS: AGFLAP

If you're like most people, your emotions and behavior have been almost totally determined by your unconscious programs and you have had very little control over your thoughts, feelings and actions.

Your "I" sense has repeatedly been overruled by these unconscious programs from the past.

As you've seen in Part One, the ability to discriminate is at the core of our ability to put our "I" sense back in charge and to change ourselves for the better.

In this part, we'll consider the negative/AGFLAP emotions, one by one. This will help you gain control over your programs and emotions by increasing your ability to discriminate so that your "I" sense can determine your behavior, rather than the programs in your subconscious being in charge.

On our chart of emotions, apathy has the lowest level of energy available for action. This is the result of the energy required to suppress all of our feelings—positive as well as negative.

Let's begin there...then we'll have no place else to go but up.

"It's no use. I can't go on. I'm too tired — weary — exhausted—drained, and for what? Nobody else cares so why should I? I guess I'm too old and too ugly and good for nothing. I might just as well sleep."

A Person in Apathy

CHAPTER 3

APATHY

APATHY: "Lack of feeling or emotion; impassiveness; lack of interest or concern; indifference."—*Webster.*

On our chart of emotions, apathy has the lowest level of energy available for action. This is the result of all our feelings—positive as well as negative—being suppressed.

This occurs because as we suppress painful, negative and uncomfortable feelings, we accumulate them in our subconscious. Once that's done, it requires more and more of our available energy to *keep* those feelings suppressed, to keep them quiet. This results in less and less energy available to us for action.

Eventually we suppress ourselves into a state of apathy. At that point, we have very little capacity or ability to discriminate and the "I" sense is almost totally obscured by the programs in our subconscious. We become unable to feel anything, good or bad, and keep ourselves in a deadened state. Our behavior reflects that lack of available energy.

For example, people in apathy will often say they are "too

tired" or "drained." They might tend to sleep a lot.

Apathetic people are also very negative. If you make a constructive or optimistic statement, they'll tend to refute it. Their overall attitude is, "You can't fight City Hall, so why bother?"

Apathy is also inertia, which is the tendency of a body at rest to remain at rest, and the tendency of a body in motion to remain in motion. Therefore, you'll find people in apathy going to work, eating, sleeping, getting married, getting divorced, having children — going through all the motions, but without any real enjoyment.

Or they'll continue an activity long beyond its usefulness. We sometimes refer to that as "being in a rut."

Some people have their home base in apathy. This is where their "I" sense comes through most of the time. They're generally tired and cynical, believing that things will never get any better, so there's no use trying.

It's important to know, however, that even when individuals have their home base in another emotional energy state, there will be occasional dips into apathy. The difference with those people is that, with their overall energy level farther up the emotional chart, they won't stay in apathy for any appreciable length of time. For example, you might hear someone who is very productive and energetic say, "That was my best shot and it didn't work. That's it—I quit!" However, they don't really mean it and the next moment, that person is saying, "All right, let's review it. That didn't work—what can we try now?" The person is in action again, working to resolve the problem.

Remember, too, that the length of time it takes for a person to get moving again will depend on how far up the emotional energy chart his or her home base is. That might be a gauge to help you in determining your home base. (Your home base means the emotional level where you are most of the time.)

If your home base is in apathy, you may *never* try anything again.

If your home base is in fear, you might hesitate for a long time before you feel safe enough to move again.

If your home base is in courageousness, you'll rebound quickly, perhaps only in seconds or minutes.

Whatever your home base is, apathy will probably be part of your makeup as long as you have any suppressed feelings. However, as you eliminate the negative feelings, you'll tend to move up the chart of emotions and after a while, your apathy attacks will lessen in intensity and duration.

It's also important to remember that you might be on different energy levels in the various areas of your life. You could be in courageousness in your career, yet be totally unable to cope with a particular relationship or with your child's problems in school. And when that difficult area comes up, you could drop into grief or apathy.

(Note: This can be confusing when you begin to look at the whole picture of your emotional life, because it might seem that you're in one emotional state when it is really something else entirely. The chapter, "Find Your Home Base" will help you discriminate. It gives you some ideas of what apathy and the other emotional energy states look like from an attitudinal and behavioral point of view.)

Apathy is at the bottom on our chart of emotions. In fact, it is sometimes difficult to see it as an emotion at all, because it really seems more like the absence of feelings. It's an extreme sense of "I can't," where we feel numb, deadened or defeated. Perhaps it will be better if we think of apathy as an emotional state, rather than an emotion. It is the state we reach when we've given up—given up to such an extent that we're convinced the feelings will do us no good anyway, so there's no use in having them.

We can no longer put other people down with our pride;
    we can't force them with our anger;
    we can't seduce them with our lust;
    we can't stop them with our fear;
    we can't get their sympathy with our grief.

So we play dead in our apathy. Maybe we can at least get the world to leave us alone.

Apathy is an extreme feeling that we have no control over our lives and whatever it is that bothers us, whether it be a career change, the workplace, one's home life, mate, children, the world situation, or anything else. This may provide a clue to helping ourselves out of an apathy attack when it occurs. Find an activity where you feel in control, such as exercise or a sport you do fairly well. There are also some other suggestions for you to try in the "Remedies" section which follows. Some of the activities mentioned there could be done on your lunch hour or on weekends.

If we look for and encourage ourselves and others in those areas where we can be in control, it could go a long way toward apathy prevention.

If you're not in apathy yourself, perhaps you know someone who is and would like to help them. For example, you could offer to go for a walk with a friend or loved one who is having a problem. This would get them into action and, at the same time, give them someone to talk to about what's bothering them if they're open to that.

In the case of young people, teenagers, for example, parents could help by giving these young persons control over certain areas of life such as curfew, bedtime, choice of TV programs, decorating their own rooms or space in any manner they choose, wearing the clothes they like, and other such decisions. Even if the parents are not in total agreement with some of those choices, it would be worth the effort to talk together and decide which areas they could be flexible about. It could make for a happier, more self-confident young person.

For older people, a friend or counselor could help them find areas in which they can be in control. For example, volunteering in a hospital would put them in a position of being in control. There, they are able to care for others who are more out of control than they are.

Being In Control Is The Key   This concept of putting the individual into a position of control covers a wide range of options. By looking at the activities which therapists, advisors and other resources often suggest to people, and which work, you'll begin to see how each of them fits into this idea. Putting the person into a position of control seems to be the bottom line.

Some Examples—Prisoners were found to be less depressed and less antagonistic when they were given the freedom to plant a garden and choose what they would put in it.
—Some New York City neighborhoods were upgraded by allowing artistic residents to paint pictures on the walls of vacant buildings. This gave them some control over what their world looked like.
—Some residents were also given permission to create vegetable and flower gardens of their own choosing in vacant land. Those who chose to participate were each assigned a small plot of land within a fenced area and could grow whatever they wanted.
I'm sure you can think of many more examples that would illustrate what I'm suggesting here. And you can begin to see how being in control provides the key to helping people move out of an apathy emotional state.

Typical Apathy Feelings
Numb, cold, disinterested, forgetful, careless, inattentive, confused, deadened, defeated.

APATHY REMEDIES

Do Something. Do something even if you have to force yourself to get into action. This will put you in control of your energy and you'll start to feel better.

Take A Walk. This exercise is one of the best things you can do to maintain your health, physical as well as emotional. And more important, it gives you an opportunity to look around at your world and see what you can do to contribute to it. You may find things you can do while you're out. Perhaps you'll see a paper the wind has blown onto the sidewalk. You can take control of your world by picking it up and throwing it in the trash. Look for things like that which will give some purpose to your walk and make it enjoyable for you, rather than its being another chore you'd rather avoid. You might make it a game to do at least one such thing each day.

You might also find a stopping place along the way. Perhaps there's a bus stop bench where you can rest for a moment—or a coffee shop you can go into for refreshment. You might have a little friendly conversation with the server or the counter person. This will give you something to look forward to each day.

Call Someone. It helps to talk to another person, even if the conversation is not an important one. You could just call someone to say hello, or to suggest watching television or seeing a movie together.

Go To The Park. This gets you out into nature, which can give you quite a lift. Sitting on a park bench in summer, watching the people go by, feeding the birds, relaxing, looking at the trees and flowers can be wonderful to get you out of the depression of apathy. And in the wintertime, a brisk walk in the cold air is terrific for blowing the cobwebs out of your mind.

Eat Out. Again, this gets you out into the world where you can relate to people. Even if you should get annoyed or upset with a person while you're out, it is still an improvement over the deadness of apathy.

Do Something For Someone Else. This is one of the best ways of getting rid of apathy because it gives you some purpose to your life. It doesn't have to be a big thing you do, either. For instance, you might help a handicapped person who is afraid to cross the street—or hold a bag of groceries while someone opens the car door. You could look for this kind of thing to do while you're on your walk. Another good idea is to volunteer for some charitable activity once or twice a week if your time allows.

Get Yourself A Pet. Having another being to take care of is one of the best ways to help yourself. You might want to choose an animal which doesn't require much attention, such as a bird or hamster. Or you might prefer a cat, or even a dog to accompany you on your walks. The local Humane Society or the classified section of the newspaper will often offer free pets to a good home.

Be Pleasant To Others. Try it, even if you don't mean it at first. After a while, you might even start being nice to yourself.

A Further Note. These remedies are great to try whether apathy is your home base, or if you're just having a temporary apathy attack. They'll get you into action and that will help either way.

In the meanwhile, let's move on up the energy chart to grief. I'll bet you never thought of grief as a step up from anything before. Maybe that's why they call it "good grief."

NOTES

NOTES

"It hurts so much, I can't stand it. If only someone could understand how I feel and help me. I wouldn't be a burden, I'd be good, if only somebody would please love me and take care of me. Please."

A Person in Grief

CHAPTER 4

GRIEF

GRIEF: "Intense emotional suffering caused by loss, misfortune, injury, or evils of any kind; sorrow; regret."—*Webster.*

Grief is the next energy level above apathy and it has a little more energy available for action. Its nature is painful; it hurts; and most often, our action is to cry.

The reason it's painful is that we're moving up out of apathy where our emotions are dead, numb, asleep, and the energy is stopped. In grief, the energy is beginning to flow but with tremendous constriction; it hurts; and that is the emotion which we call grief. Have you ever had a hand or foot go to sleep? Remember how it felt when it started to wake up again? Pins and needles; often very painful. Grief is this kind of experience in an emotional sense.

With regard to the amount of energy available to us in the state of grief, we can usually carry on limited and often aimless activities. As an example, a woman who has suffered a deep loss might dust the same piece of furniture over and over again, or keep putting more sugar into her coffee, without being aware of what she was doing.

In grief, there is such lack of discrimination that we may even be unaware of our surroundings. Our attention is almost totally turned within, focused on our pain and helplessness. This causes us to be unaware of and unconcerned about other people and the effect our emotional state might be having on them.

However, we don't perceive ourselves as being unconcerned. And if others complain about our attitude or behavior, we usually feel that *they* don't care about us and that they aren't even trying to understand what we're going through.

An important point to remember is that every feeling, including grief, represents energy being suppressed and under pressure. From the moment that energy is suppressed, it is trying to expend itself—while we apply tremendous pressure to prevent that from happening. When the pressure builds up and we can't keep it suppressed any longer, it bursts through as an expression of the feeling. If we're in grief, we'll cry. If we're in anger, we'll shout. The expressing of emotion occurs because the suppressed energy has to push through the holding energy in order to relieve the pressure.

If you would consciously decide to stop holding that energy down, it would quickly, easily and harmlessly expend itself without the necessity to express it on others. This is because the energy itself is neutral. It only becomes destructive when we suppress it, and the more tightly we try to hold it, the more explosive it is when it finally pushes through. We find ourselves stuck between the pressure from within (which is the feeling trying to expend itself) and our efforts to suppress it again.

YOU GET STUCK! What can you do? With grief, it often helps to have a good cry, keeping the thought in mind that you're doing it to unsuppress and to expend the energy, and not just to indulge the grief. In this way, you'll stop trying to keep it suppressed and some of the energy will go out.

One problem with letting your emotions flow and starting to cry is your unconscious wish to keep all the feelings suppressed and out of your conscious awareness. This could make it difficult for you to cry because you might feel out of control when you do. Usually people in grief will either fight the feeling or wallow in it. Only occasionally will they simply use the expressing of it as a means to let go of the feelings. On those rare occasions when they do that, when they stop fighting the feeling and just decide to let it happen, they feel immensely better afterward. It's because they've allowed a bit of the energy to expend itself without fighting it.

So don't wallow in grief! And don't fight it! Simply allow the pressure behind the feeling to push it up and out! You'll feel much better afterward.

Typical Grief Feelings
Sad, unhappy, bereaved, lonely, hurt, wounded, tormented, tearful, melancholy.

GRIEF REMEDIES

Have A Good Cry. Decide that you're going to cry, rather than crying because you can't help yourself. Decide that you're going to allow yourself the luxury of crying. Now I don't mean a wimpy little cry, although that's all right to begin with if that's the best you can do at first. No, I mean a really good cry. Find a quiet place where you won't be disturbed and let it go. And while you're crying, think about the fact that YOU'RE DOING IT — IT'S NOT CONTROLLING YOU, YOU'RE CONTROLLING IT. Think about allowing that suppressed energy to flow up and out through your tears—and about how you're letting go of all your unhappiness with every tear. You'll feel tons better when you're finished.

Talk To A Friend About What's Bothering You. This is an excellent way to start unsuppressing those thoughts and feelings which are hurting you. Sometimes you're not able to open it up enough by yourself. At those times, a good listener can help. Try to choose someone who won't start telling you how right or wrong you are—or what you should do about the situation or person—that can just make matters worse sometimes. Try to find someone who will just simply listen. Talking about it could be a big help in getting you started on your good cry, too, if you're having trouble.

Be Around Cheerful People. This is wonderful for lifting you out of a funk, especially if they can start you laughing. A good, hearty, belly laugh is a good release of pent-up energy. Sometimes, if you can do this, you won't even need the good cry. A good comedy book or movie can sometimes accomplish this also.

Do Something For Someone Else. This is a wonderful way to get your attention away from yourself and your feelings. Remember that the feelings keep you focused internally, on your problems. This activity gets you looking outward.

NOTES:

"Be careful, watch what you say. They're all out to get you and you can't trust anyone. So watch yourself and don't ever let anyone get too close."

A Person in Fear

CHAPTER 5

FEAR

FEAR: "A feeling of anxiety and agitation caused by the presence or nearness of danger, evil, pain, etc.; timidity; dread; fright; apprehension."—*Webster.*

Fear is an emotion which we also experience when there is no presence or nearness of danger, evil, or pain, but only the thought of it.

Fear is an emotional energy level which is inwardly chaotic. If you have a hot skillet on the stove, then flick drops of water into it, you're looking at an illustration of what fear feels like. The droplets dancing in the pan and fear both have a "pssst, pssst, pssst" feeling to them.

Because of its chaotic nature, fear is an emotion which we don't like to stay in. We will avoid it if we can because it is not comfortable. We'll try to escape it, suppress it, and pretend it isn't there. It shuts down our discriminators to the extreme and we often can't think what to do. Our minds go blank and we cannot take any action.

Fear is an emotion in which we also experience many types of physical responses, more than with any of the other emotions. In an attempt to suppress the feeling, we sometimes develop a tightness or knot in our mid-section. Or we might notice that our mouths are dry, our hands clammy, and we have butterflies in the stomach, or nausea.

Fear may also manifest as a general sense of anxiety which seems to pervade all our activities, even though there may be no apparent rational reason for it. Fear is an extremely debilitating emotion. It saps our strength and often puts us into a state of immobility, which is not like apathy with its heaviness and numbness, but which is more like being frozen, tense, and unable to move or make a decision.

Another quality of fear, when you move into the higher energy level of the emotion, is defensiveness. Fear is the first emotion where you will begin to take outward action to correct a situation. However, you will do it only under extreme provocation.

Needless to say, many of our subconscious survival programs come into play in the fear energy level.

Fight or Flight?

Fear seems to be a pivotal emotion because when we're in a dangerous situation (real or imaginary) and become afraid, we will either suppress the feeling, freeze, and move into apathy; or we'll move into a higher energy band of fear and run away. If flight is not possible, we'll take the defensive action necessary to protect ourselves; we'll fight.

It is very important to remember that when the emotion of fear is stirred up, we are often unable to discriminate between a real threat and an imagined danger. Therefore, if the fear feeling is intense, we may be doing things which are out of all proportion to the actual need.

Our lack of discrimination caused by emotions can and does get us into no end of trouble. The "I" sense becomes blocked; then the programs direct our behavior in sometimes foolish and embarrassing ways.

Being able to discriminate on the fear feelings themselves gives us a handle on getting rid of them.

Typical Fear Feelings

Scared, fearful, cautious, nervous, uneasy, jumpy, anxious, worried, startled.

FEAR REMEDIES

Get Out. If you suddenly find yourself in a fearful situation and you cannot discriminate, get out of the situation as fast as you can. It's better to run away and later realize that there was no real danger, than it is to keep telling yourself that there's no danger and have it turn out otherwise.

Face Your Fear Feelings. Try putting yourself gradually, for short periods of time, into situations which are safe, but where you might feel afraid. This will give you the opportunity to explore your fear feelings without any danger to yourself—and to evaluate your feelings with the idea of discriminating and getting rid of them if they're not useful.

Here's how to do this: While you're in your chosen situation, allow yourself to feel the feeling and then ask yourself if that feeling is necessary or not. Is the feeling helping you? If the answer is no, then you might notice that the feeling will diminish a bit. This is using discrimination. When you ask yourself the question, you're putting your "I" sense in charge and the feeling is not needed any more so it will usually get lighter.

For example, if you're afraid of lions, you might go to the lion house at the zoo where the animal is behind bars and cannot hurt you. As you look at the lion, you can explore your feelings and ask yourself if you need those feelings, ask if those feelings are helping you at that moment. I think you'll begin to see that the feelings are not really that necessary.

Now, you might start to think that if the lion were out of the cage, then the fear feeling would be helpful—you might think that the feeling would make you run away. But stop and think about that for a moment. Don't you think that you would have the good sense to run away from danger even without the feeling? Of course you would! And sometimes the fear feeling makes it worse because you become frozen and can't do anything at all. Then you're really stuck. Think about this when you're exploring your feelings.

You could also look at pictures of what you're afraid of in order to feel your feelings. And I want to remind you that the bottom line is you being in control, rather than the feelings pushing you around. Doing these things puts *you* in control.

Evaluate The Situation. Sit down with paper and pencil and evaluate the realities of any situations in the following way:

First: Put the thing you want to do, or are afraid of, at the top of the page. Then write down all your thoughts and considerations about it, all the things you're afraid might happen. Then go over your list and evaluate whether each item is a True, a Possible, or just a Feeling. Mark each with a T, a P, or an F. By the time you've finished, you should have a better, more realistic picture of the situation or goal.

Next: Take each item marked T or P and write down what you might do to prevent it or what you could do to handle it if it actually happened.

By the end of this evaluation, which could take anywhere from a few minutes to several days, you'll have a much clearer picture of the situation.

Avoid Dangerous Situations. If there's a possibility of danger, avoid the situation if you can.

If you can't avoid the situation, then be sure to discriminate by being aware of your feelings and asking yourself if they are helping you or not. I think that sometimes you'll find the fear getting weaker and your head getting clearer as you discriminate.

Get Into Action. Take an action about something that you don't feel fearful about. Examine your feelings while you do this. It will help you to get familiar with the feeling of confidence — and let you know that you're not a fearful person, just a person who gets afraid sometimes.

Talk About It. Talk to someone about your fears. You might be surprised to find out that the other person also gets afraid sometimes. Talking about it will also help you unsuppress your thoughts and feelings so that you can better discriminate about them. You might even want to have regular once-a-month get-togethers with some others to talk about your fears and other feelings. You can help one another by helping each other to discriminate.

Don't Feel Foolish. Decide to not feel foolish about being afraid. There's nothing to feel foolish about, even if the fear seems to be unfounded. Everyone feels afraid at times, so you're not alone.

NOTES:

NOTES:

"Give it to me! NOW! I want it and I can't wait! More! More! Hurry up! I want it so badly, I can taste it. I want it and I don't care! I just want it and I want it NOW!"

A Person in Lust

CHAPTER 6

LUST

LUST: "Overmastering desire; eagerness to possess or enjoy; a desire to gratify the senses; bodily appetite."—*Webster.*

Lust is an energy level that gets us moving. This is because when we want something badly enough, we will override our fears and move out to get it.

Look at the energy chart again. It takes about 80% of our available energy to suppress this action emotion, but we do have more energy left for action than we had in either apathy, grief or fear. If you look at the two aspects of lust you will understand why it takes so much energy to suppress it.

Lust has two parts:

I WANT

I CANNOT/SHOULD NOT HAVE

That combination is what makes it lust. Think about that for a moment. Were it not for your unconscious "cannot/should not have," you would simply think about wanting something, then you'd go and get it. And it would be easy!

Can you think of any personal examples to support that statement? For instance, have you ever wanted a drink of water while you were in your kitchen? Was it difficult to get it? No, it was easy.

Why? Because you could have it. There was no "cannot have" in the way.

Now put yourself in your car, miles from anywhere, and you're thirsty, and you want some water. What's your feeling? *Lust!* You *REALLY* want that water! You *lust for it.* The more you think about it, the more you want it and the worse you feel. Why? Because you can't have it. There's a "cannot have" in the way.

How about an example of a "should not have?" Maybe you're on a diet and "should not have" ice cream and chocolate. If you like ice cream and chocolate, what happens when you think about a hot fudge sundae? *Lust!* Some people can't stop thinking about it and eventually go on a binge and off the diet. Years ago, the only diet that my father was ever able to stay with long enough to lose weight was one where he was instructed to eat anything he wanted on one day each week. Do you see how that helped him? They removed the "should not have," which prevented the lust feelings from pushing him out of control.

The "cannot/should not have" part makes it especially frustrating because, with that feeling, even when we get something, we still feel that we can't have it. We don't believe it's ours, we don't believe we can keep it, we don't feel it's enough. Because of our inner feelings of want, deprivation, guilt and lack, nothing satisfies or fulfills us no matter how much we may acquire. Therefore, we're frequently driven to keep eating or acquiring things long past any real need.

An example of this is Thanksgiving dinner. We may overeat with the excuse that it's only once a year. If you examine that statement, you see the implication of "cannot have." The feeling behind it is that the food will be taken away and you won't be able to have it again until next year. That's a long time to wait! Unconsciously you begin to feel threatened with deprivation, so you'll eat as much as you can while you have the chance.

And because you "cannot have" it, you don't really enjoy it. In fact, you may not even be fully aware of the taste. You end up overfull, not really satisfied and you may even still feel hungry. A friend of mine used to refer to this as "mouth hungry," rather than "stomach hungry."

On the other hand, have you ever snacked later on the leftovers of the Thanksgiving feast? Did you notice how relaxed you felt then, and how good it tasted? That's because the once-a-year feast was over, you could relax and allow yourself to *HAVE* the food. At that point, you could really taste it in a way that is impossible when you're driven by the "cannot have" of lust.

Now, we're not often aware of the "cannot have" part because our focus is on the intense wanting, and that's the feeling we experience. Desire, possessiveness, envy, greed are some words which describe the feeling and belong in the lust group of feelings.

There's also a lot of guilt associated with the "should not have" element of lust. There's a sense that we're not supposed to have; we're not even supposed to want. This is particularly true with the indulgence of bodily appetites, perhaps because of cultural views.

When we were young, most of us were taught by parents, teachers and friends to suppress our lust feelings, our wants. They didn't do it maliciously, but that hardly matters. The damage was done anyway, and the end result is the same. We often feel guilty and ashamed for wanting anything for ourselves. Consequently we either hide the fact that we want something, or subconsciously we cannot allow ourselves to have it. And when we do break through and get something we want, often we won't let ourselves enjoy it. Some people even give all their things away because of their guilt and "cannot/should not have" programs buried in their subconscious.

Can you remember being told as a child,

"Don't be so selfish," or

"Don't be greedy" or

"Don't be so pushy, wait your turn"?

These are some examples of how we can be taught (programmed) to suppress our wanting. These programs influence us our entire lives and we have a lot of feelings about that.

It's important to remember that there's nothing wrong with wanting. Watch children. You'll see that as a child, it's natural to reach out for what you want. It doesn't occur to you that you can't have it, therefore you're not inhibited at that stage of your life.

As you get more and more negative responses or "No's," as well as getting disapproval for asking for certain things, you might conclude that you'll be better off and better liked if you hide your desires and feelings of wanting. You begin to suppress them.

And when the same feelings and desires that you're trying to suppress keep coming back over and over again, you may start to feel guilty. After a while, you start to disapprove of yourself. Then you have to suppress even harder in order to live with yourself.

You might also come to the conclusion that you'll be safer if you don't want what someone else has. This tends to increase your motivation to suppress your feelings.

In addition to everything else, there's a tremendous conflict in lust. *Unconsciously,* you think lust is negative, and *consciously,* you think it's positive.

You think it's *negative* because you've been told that wanting pleasurable things is bad.

You think it's *positive* because you anticipate a forthcoming pleasure.

Also, the more you anticipate the pleasure and the closer you get to having it, the greater is your feeling of lust.

It's no wonder that our society is confused on the subject today where there's such a strong emphasis on the sex aspect of lust and on "letting it all hang out." This current push to expose those feelings, coupled with your intense past programming to suppress the whole thing, can sometimes create more problems than it solves.

It will help for you to discriminate and to understand what lust is and how it fits into the whole emotional energy picture. Then and only then will these conflicts begin to make sense to you.

The Positive Side To Lust

It's also important to realize that there's a *positive* side to lust. What is it? Wanting motivates us into action.

There is an energy in the lust emotion which allows us to get out of our self-imposed shell. When the want for something is strong enough and intense enough, we will overcome our "cannot/should not have's," and move to attain that which we desire.

And the anticipation of pleasure causes the lust feelings to increase. This results in being willing to use a higher energy level to overcome the obstacles!

In short, it is the first AGFLAP emotion where we have the energy to aggressively reach out for something. Therefore, it's important to recognize that you have those feelings within yourself and to acknowledge them without judgment. Do that and you'll be on your way to eliminating the "cannot/should not have" feelings connected with lust. You'll find that you can have more, and enjoy it, too.

And if you're willing to recognize and deal with your lust feelings, you'll be more discriminating as to whether the thing desired is good for you or bad for you, whether you really want it or not, whether it's worth pursuing, whether you're ready to spend the time and energy required to obtain it, and so forth.

Typical Lust Feelings

Greedy, hungry, desirous, driven, compulsive, ruthless, insensitive.

LUST REMEDIES

Observe Yourself. Begin to notice how you feel when you get something you want. Do you feel guilty? If so, you'll be an unconscious saboteur, undermining your ability to have and to do. If that's the case, notice the guilt feeling and ask yourself if you really need to feel that way. Whatever you answer is okay. Just asking and answering the question will allow you to discriminate and put you more in control. You might also notice that some of the guilt feeling will lift.

Let Yourself Have. Begin with some small thing you would like but feel that you should not have. It might be some dessert, for instance. Decide that you will allow yourself to have the dessert—and this is the hard part—allow yourself to really enjoy it. Decide that you will fully taste each and every bite, and observe how you feel as you go along. If you notice any of those uncomfortable, guilty feelings, stop eating for a moment and concentrate on the feeling, whatever it is. Talk to the feeling...tell it that you appreciate its reminding you not to eat too much but that you have the situation under control. Tell it that you've decided to have the dessert, and that you're going to enjoy it and that the feeling is not going to stop you, so it might just as well go away and stop bothering you. Then continue to eat. I think you'll be surprised at how well this approach works.

Now, you might worry that if you enjoy it so much, you'll want to keep on eating more and more. But the opposite is true. It's only when you deny yourself the enjoyment of what you're having, so that you feel deprived, that you have to keep on having more. When you *really* enjoy something, you need less of it.

You can also use this on other things besides food. Maybe you'd like to buy a new pair of shoes, or move to a nicer house, or treat yourself to a massage, or get a better job. Well, I would say to go ahead and do it as long as it's not being done to hurt someone else, and it won't be harmful to yourself.

Allow Yourself To Dream. This is an important remedy to open you up to things you've wanted, but that you might have given up on. Set aside some time each day for dreaming. It doesn't have to be a long time, maybe only 5 or 10 minutes in the morning or evening, but it should be time when you're not rushed and can just relax and dream about all the things you want. You can write some of these dreams down too, if you like, but even if you don't want to do that, dreaming about what you want will help.

While you dream, you can also notice your feelings and tell them that they are not going to stop you from dreaming, and they're not going to stop you from having what you want. Tell them they can go away now because you've got everything under control. At the same time, see if you can let them go out of your mind and out of you.

Make A Collage. Go through magazines and cut out pictures of what you would like to have. Then get a large sheet of posterboard and rubber cement from an art supply store. Use the rubber cement to glue the pictures onto the posterboard, making a collage.

Explore your creative nature by making the collage as colorful and artistically pleasing as possible. Put this where you can see it once in a while. It will help by reminding you of your goals.

Evaluate Your Wants. Make a "want list." Put down everything you can think of that you've wanted to have or do in the past year or so. Also include things you might have wanted in the past but forgot about because you thought you couldn't have them.

Then go over the list, item by item, and ask yourself the following questions:

a) Do I really want it?
b) Would it be good for me to have it or do it?
c) Would it be hurtful to someone else if I have it or do it?
d) How would I feel if I got it or did it?
e) If I had it right now, how would I feel?
f) If I had it right now, would I want to keep it?
g) What would I need to give up in order to get it?
        in terms of time?
        in terms of energy?
        in terms of family and friends?
        in terms of my own principles?
h) Am I willing to do what's necessary to get it?

Answering these questions may help you make a decision regarding each item — either a decision to go for it — or a decision to forget it. Whichever you decide, you'll be that much further ahead. You will have moved away a step from being run by your subconscious programs, to conscious control of your life.

NOTES:

"Get out of my way or I'll kill you. I hate you, you creep, you dummy, you idiot...I'll clobber you good and then mop up the street with your head. So don't touch me... don't even come near me...I'm dangerous!"

A Person in Anger

CHAPTER 7

ANGER

ANGER: "A strong feeling excited by a real or supposed injury; often accompanied by a desire to take vengeance, or to obtain satisfaction from the offending party; resentment; wrath; ire."—*Webster.*

As you can see on the energy chart, people in anger are using less energy to suppress than they did in the apathy through lust emotions, and they have more energy available for action. However, the energy in the anger state is so intense and destructive that the anger behavior is also destructive. And when anger takes over completely, we could kill. We blindly want to destroy everyone and everything in our path.

In anger, we often feel that we have to attack. We feel we must destroy before we are destroyed.

Anger is an energy which we try to suppress and keep suppressed because we're afraid of it. We don't feel safe when we're angry. We feel that we could lose control and hurt ourselves or others. Consequently, we don't feel safe when anyone else is angry, because we think they could lose control and hurt us.

And what happens when we suppress those anger feelings? We move ourselves down the energy chart to grief or apathy, where it may feel safe. The problem is that although we may *feel* safer in those lower energy states, they are actually very limited, unfree, non-energetic and non-productive states.

Furthermore, when some of us get to apathy, we program ourselves into behaving nicely as a way of hiding the fact that we have hostile, angry feelings which we're keeping suppressed. We even try to hide the anger feelings from ourselves, and after a while, may convince ourselves that we don't really have them at all. After that, we're even more careful to keep our anger under cover.

People who have done this might think that they never get angry, yet they are not always kind or nice people. Their actions reflect a non-loving attitude, and when you're around them, you may notice that you don't feel good, in spite of their seemingly sweet attitude.

Some people will even boast that they never get angry. And in some cases, they're so good at suppressing that if someone provokes them, they'll try to rationalize that person's behavior so as to keep their anger feelings from surfacing. They'll make excuses for the other person, such as, "He didn't really mean it," or "She doesn't know what she's doing." Nevertheless, even with this type of rationalization, there is often an uneasiness or inner churning at those times.

The negative emotions take a tremendous toll in terms of happiness and well-being. Many members of the medical community are beginning to explore the concept that emotional stress is a contributing cause in much of the extreme suffering people experience on a physical level. They're finding that this can manifest itself in heart attacks, ulcers, high blood pressure, drug abuse, addictions, burn-out and other illnesses, large and small.

Another area where emotions are a contributing factor is in the epidemic number of abuse incidents getting so much publicity these days. Child abuse, spousal abuse, parental abuse, incest, crimes of violence against strangers, incidents of senseless mass violence are all manifestations of negative programs taking over and pushing people into destructive behavior.

But all of this doesn't happen in a day. It begins when we're babies and builds up over time by our continuing to suppress the feelings day by day, week by week, month by month, year by year. We ignore the warning signs, sometimes not even aware of what those warning signs are.

It can be a tremendous shock to us when something happens that literally blows our cover. We might go out of control and do things which we deeply regret. We might feel terribly guilty and determine that we will never allow that kind of thing to happen again. We might even make promises to the injured party to that effect, and with all good intentions. We work harder to suppress the feelings.

Then, a week or a month or a year later, it happens again. How do we feel then? More remorseful, more guilty, more frightened and more determined to never let it happen again. We suppress even harder.

Then it happens again. What do we do now? Some people go for help, others withdraw even more into their shell of frustration and fear of themselves and those monster feelings which they begin to believe are their true nature.

We need to learn to get rid of our destructive feelings, not just keep on suppressing them. Sometimes others can help us do this in an organized or professional manner. The Sedona Method is such a way. It is an actual how-to technique for eliminating feelings. There's more about it at the end of this book.

But the first thing you must do is begin to recognize the truth! Those monster feelings are not your true nature, no matter how it may appear. They are only feelings and, as such, can be eliminated.

And if you're one of those people who say that they never get angry, I'm going to present an idea that you might like to think about. Please remember that this is a general statement. It may not apply to every person who appears to fit this description.

In general, those who say they never feel angry or those who never express any anger might be more dangerous in the long run than those who are able to express their anger freely, without hurting anyone.

For example, a man who can say what's on his mind when he doesn't like something you've done is much less likely to take out a gun and shoot you for that thing. Once again, this is a general statement.

Of course, there are those people who say what's on their minds, and you know that you'd better watch your step with them because the next time, you'll get a punch. But somehow, in those cases, they're still safer because they're giving you warning of the danger. Whereas those who hold it all in and don't say anything are liable to explode when you least expect it.

Do you remember what's been said about some of the people who've exploded into senseless and mass violence? Neighbors and others who knew them often commented that they couldn't believe it, because the killer was so soft-spoken and gentle, always wished them a good morning and never did anything to disturb or bother anyone. Until, of course, the killings.

So, to repeat, in general, those who say they never feel angry or who never express anger might be more dangerous in the long run than those who express it freely. The fact that they never allow themselves to feel any anger may be an indication that they're afraid they can't handle it.

People who have their home base in anger find it easier to express it, and are in a higher energy level, than those who keep it suppressed. They can express their anger without physically hurting anyone. They are often high achievers, even though it may not always be pleasant to work for them or to be around them because they'll usually tell you what's on their minds, whether you like it or not.

Nevertheless, in spite of their outbursts, they are usually safer to be with than the person in apathy, because they actually have less suppressed anger and hostility. That's why they don't have to be afraid of the anger emotion.

In the overall, they're freer, and most people would rather be around them with their outbursts, than to be with someone who's in apathy and won't even talk or discuss the problems.

So what can you do about your anger feelings? Well, if you can discriminate and recognize that they are only feelings arising from past programs, your "I" sense might then make a decision to not be run by those past programs. Then, when the anger feelings arise, you might choose not to let the program push you into undesirable behavior. You might choose to divert that energy into a harmless activity such as running or sports.

The key to freedom is discrimination...the ability to see things as they are. With discrimination, you recognize that the emotions are nothing more than present manifestations of past programs. That understanding gives you power over the feelings.

With discrimination, your "I" sense is in control.

Typical Anger Feelings
Hatred, spite, resentment, pushiness, fury, mad, hot under the collar, enraged.

ANGER REMEDIES

Divert Your Energy Into A Harmless Activity. It is important that your "I" sense begins to take charge of your behavior, rather than you being run by your past programs. This is especially true in the anger feelings because they are so terribly destructive and can hurt others as well as yourself. If you express the feelings on others, the others are hurt—if you keep suppressing the feelings and holding all that destructiveness inside of yourself, *you* end up being hurt. So when you get angry, see if you can hold everything until you can expend some of the energy in a way that won't hurt anybody. Some things you can do are:

> take a run
> punch a punching bag
> punch a pillow
> work out at the gym
> play tennis
> hit golf balls at a driving range
> ride a bicycle

While you're involved in the activity, try to think of yourself as letting go of the anger energy, rather than simply expressing it. Keep reminding yourself that your "I" sense is in charge, not your feelings, and that you are choosing to do this activity instead of doing something destructive. After a while, you'll begin to feel more in control of yourself and less at the mercy of the emotions and programs from the past.

Communicate Your Feelings. Allow yourself to communicate your feelings when it's appropriate. This could work well at times when you're only annoyed or upset, rather than waiting until you're really angry and out of control. Try talking to the other person about what's bothering you. Try not to blame them for *your* feelings because that would only stir up *their* anger feelings, their discriminator would shut down, and it would be much more difficult for them to really hear you. During the discussion, keep yourself aware of your feelings and if the anger (yours or theirs) seems to be building and getting out of control, get out of there fast and try another remedy.

Write To The Person. Write a letter to the person you're angry with—but don't send it. Write it for yourself. This is another way for you to harmlessly expend some of your anger energy, and it gives you the opportunity to express all of your angry feelings, without jeopardizing your relationship with that person. If necessary, you could write a letter every day for a while, until you get it all out.

You can also read the letter or letters later on. A good question to ask yourself when you do that is, "Do I have to feel this way?" Frequently, you'll realize that whatever you were angry about is no longer important. You might even have a good laugh over it then. This remedy is especially good because it gives you the opportunity to later discriminate and see the whole thing in a more realistic perspective.

Write A Letter About The Situation. You may or may not send this one. If it's about a public issue, you might want to send it to the editor of your newspaper. If it's about a personal situation, then you might just want to write it for yourself.

Talk About Your Feelings. Talk to someone about your feelings. This is another way for you to express some of those angry feelings in a harmless way that won't hurt anyone. "Getting it off your chest" might be just the relief you need.

If you don't feel comfortable talking to a friend about

these feelings, you might want to consult your priest, minister or rabbi or a good therapist. They're used to dealing with those kinds of problems, without making judgments about you as a person. Or you might want to take the Sedona Method Course to learn how to eliminate negative feelings. Whatever you decide to do, the important thing is for you to get some help if you feel that your anger is getting out of control.

Talk To Yourself. Talk to yourself about your feelings. This is a good one when you're driving, or when you're home alone. Remember that the idea is not to indulge the feelings, but to get your discriminator working so that your "I" sense can take charge. You might ask yourself some questions, such as,

"Did I do anything to create or contribute to this situation or problem?"

"Is there anything I can do that would help to resolve or alleviate this situation or problem?"

And, if the answer is yes,

"Am I willing to do it?"

Ask For Help. Don't be ashamed to ask for help. Whatever the problem is, someone, somewhere, sometime, has had the very same problem—and has been helped through it. You can be, too!

NOTES:

"You've really got to do something about that smug, superior attitude of yours. It just doesn't work with me. You've got to realize that I am the best...everyone knows that...and you'll probably never catch up. But you can keep trying...and you should. You'll never make it, of course, but at least you can keep your little self busy."

A Person in Pride

CHAPTER 8

PRIDE

PRIDE: "An overhigh opinion of oneself; exaggerated self-esteem; conceit."—*Webster.*

If you know someone who thinks that it's impossible to have an overhigh opinion of him or herself, that person is probably in pride.

The funny thing about pride is that it can also work the other way, such as the person who tries to be *worse* than anyone else, or meaner, or uglier, or more stupid. There's also a pride in that.

Pride is a holding energy level. People in pride have accomplished something and they want to be recognized for it.

At the same time, they don't want to be challenged by someone doing them "one better" so they try to hold others back.

Look again at the energy level chart: Suppression and action levels are nearly equal.

Prideful people will often be cutting and nasty in manner as a way of putting others down; i.e., pushing them to a lower place on the energy chart. This is the result of a sub-conscious sense of "I can't."

People in pride often have a secret belief that their accomplishments are flukes and that they could never repeat them. Or they believe that it was just dumb luck and that others may somehow find them out. Therefore, they'll put on a show of superiority to keep people intimidated. That way, no one will think to look for a crack in the pedestal.

Another thing about the state of pride is that we're so busy holding onto the accomplishments we've achieved that we prevent ourselves from moving forward and achieving more.

How long we hold onto these things is determined by where we have our home base on the emotional energy scale. For example:

Individuals whose home base is apathy will hold on for years, always reminding people of their moment of glory, even though they might have done nothing else since. An example of this would be the high school or college baseball star who has long ago stopped playing, yet who brags about all his old school triumphs every chance he gets.

In a lust home base, such persons would hold on until the next desire becomes intense enough to force them into action.

In an anger home base, they'd be prodded into accomplishing more in a relatively short time, because they'd get angry thinking that someone else might pass them up.

QUESTION: Are you saying that pride is bad?

ANSWER: No, I'm not saying that pride is bad! On the contrary, I'm saying that, in general, pride is good because it represents achievement! Look again at the energy level chart. In the state of pride, it shows a high level of energy available for action.

QUESTION: Then what's the problem?

ANSWER: The problem is that most people get stuck in pride for a long time and it holds them back!

As you can imagine, prideful people are not very willing to look at their feelings; therefore, they don't stand much chance of getting rid of them.

They are also in the awkward position of believing that no one can tell them anything and so they're not very open to new ideas. The "I" sense becomes very much identified with the egotistical superiority feelings and the person finds it difficult, if not impossible, to bend.

Because of these attitudes and feelings, it is very difficult for the prideful person to make significant breakthroughs even though he or she may be in a high and powerful emotional energy level much of the time. Their image of themselves must always be preserved, no matter what it costs. You can see why pride is one of the biggest blocks to personal growth.

Typical Prideful Feelings

Smug, complacent, superior, condescending, presumptuous, critical, holier-than-thou, egotistical.

PRIDE REMEDIES

Be Alert. Begin to notice times when you feel prideful. And when you notice yourself behaving in a prideful way, be sure you don't put yourself down for it...simply decide to be finished with that emotional response and behavior.

Remember, I said *prideful* — not *proud* of yourself for some good deed or quality. The difference between the two is very important. When you start looking for your pridefulness, it's easy to become confused and think you should put yourself down all the time and not take credit for your accomplishments. That kind of false humility is actually a subtle form of the destructive pride or pridefulness.

Discrimination is the key. If you're discriminating and can see things clearly *as they are,* you'll be willing to recognize and acknowledge your own *good* qualities as well as your shortcomings.

Evaluate Yourself. Do a self-evaluation by writing down what you see as your positive qualities and your negative qualities. You can put a line down the middle of a sheet of paper and make a column for each.

Be honest with yourself. You might even like to put a date on it and repeat it every six months or so for self-evaluation and to keep track of your progress.

Develop A Sense Of Equality. See if you can begin to experience a sense of equality with others—a *real* equality, not a condescending attitude. In true equality there is a loving feeling toward others, rather than a critical, putting-down attitude.

Notice Who You Like. Observe the people you associate with and feel comfortable with most of the time. See if you recognize any pridefulness in them. If you do perceive them to be prideful, then there is probably a smidgen of pride in you, too.

Notice Who You Dislike. Observe the people you dislike. Look to see if they're prideful. Sometimes, what we dislike in other people are those qualities which we don't want to admit are in ourselves.

Take Criticism Constructively. If someone criticizes you or something you've done, see if you can discriminate. Rather than letting your pride get in the way of your learning from that criticism, decide to see if there's any truth in what they've said. Examine it carefully and if you see areas where their criticism has been well founded, make the necessary changes, if possible. And if the particular item or situation cannot be corrected, don't beat up on yourself and drop down into a lower energy level—simply determine to learn from the error.

If there is no objective merit in what the person has said, then look to see if you were showing off or putting them down in a prideful way. This is often a reason for criticism. The other person feels put down, moves into the anger level, and retaliates by criticizing. If this is the case, be sure not to blame them or dismiss what they've said lightly. There is no personal growth in blaming or putting down another person. Rather, use it as an indication of prideful feelings to be corrected within you.

Pride in your accomplishments is constructive and helpful. It causes you to maintain good standards of quality in whatever you do.

Pridefulness is rigid, unbending, unhearing, unreceptive, unconstructive and painful. It is not a comfortable or happy state.

Give Others Credit. Be willing to give credit to others for what they've accomplished. The prideful person usually has trouble in wholeheartedly acknowledging others for their accomplishments or good qualities. Oh, they may say something nice about someone, but will then add a put-down of some kind such as, "You really did a good job on that—for a person without a college degree," or "You look so young—did you have a face lift?" If you catch yourself doing this one, just decide to leave off the last part of the sentence. You'll be a much happier person.

Look For The Positive. Look for positive qualities in others. Everyone has them, but if you're a prideful person, you're more interested in finding the negative in others because that's one of the ways you think you can protect yourself. Start discriminating and keep reminding yourself that you don't need to protect yourself that way anymore. It may seem difficult at first but if you persist, you'll become a much happier person.

Now that we've covered the negative or AGFLAP emotions in Part Two, we'll move on in Part Three to the positive feelings, the ones that are constructive and uplifting and that inspire happiness.

Notes:

"Happiness is our inherent, natural state. The best definition for happiness is peace, tranquility, and serenity. Happiness is the absence of apathy, grief, fear, jealousy, anger and hate. Happiness is loving. Happiness is freedom; absence of limitations. The less limited we are, the freer we are—and the happier we are."

Lester Levenson.

PART THREE

THE POSITIVE EMOTIONS: CAP

Happiness is you being you. It is you minus your AGFLAP.

Contrary to what many people think, it takes no special effort to be happy. It is actually the easiest thing in the world because what could be easier than just being yourself?

But, because of their AGFLAP, most people have to try very hard to be happy. They spend a lot of time and energy acquiring things or doing things which they believe will *make* them happy. They don't know how to simply *allow* themselves to be happy.

Well, if happiness is you being you, then there must be a way for you to be who you are. And there is! It's to get rid of what you're *not,* to get rid of your unhappiness, to get rid of your AGFLAP.

You see, it all has to do with feelings. Happiness is a feeling. Unhappiness is also a feeling. Observe yourself when you're happy and when you're unhappy and ask yourself the following questions:

1. *When you're happy, ask, "Where do I feel the happiness?"*
2. *When you're unhappy, ask, "Where do I feel the unhappiness?"*

You'll probably notice that you feel it inside yourself. Now, it's important to stop thinking about what you believe made you happy or unhappy. *Simply observe the state of happiness or unhappiness as though you are a totally self-contained unit of creation.* Once you've achieved that perspective, try the following:

If you're *happy,* concentrate on the feeling of happiness and ask yourself if it's possible for you to *continue* feeling happy.

If you're *unhappy,* concentrate on the feeling of unhappiness and ask yourself if it's possible for you to *stop* feeling unhappy?

Try it! The results will surprise you.

"Of course I can—and so can you. And don't ever let anyone tell you otherwise. It's just a matter of persistence. All you need to do is decide that you want it, then go for it. And I'm behind you all the way because I know you can do it."

A Person in Courageousness

CHAPTER 9

COURAGEOUSNESS

COURAGEOUSNESS: "The quality of being fearless or brave; valor; pluck."—*Webster.*

What Is Courageousness?

Please take a moment to think of how you would answer that question. The idea is to explore it for yourself before going on. In this way, you'll be giving yourself an opportunity to weigh your own thinking against someone else's opinion. The more complete you make your answer, the better frame of reference you'll have for comparison. You'd be surprised at how many people never give themselves a chance to think about such things. I'm going to leave some space here so you can write your definition if you wish.

COURAGEOUSNESS IS _____

_____

_____

_____

What did you answer? You might have said, "Courageousness is an attribute of a person who is afraid to do something but does it anyway." For example, some people are afraid of flying, but they'll take a plane anyway because of the time it saves. Well, you might say that that person has courage...and you would be correct.

But the criterion for courage in this case is not in the fact that the person is afraid. If you look again at Mr. Webster's definition, you'll see that courageousness is the quality of being fearless.

So in the above instance, what is it that makes it courageousness? It is that in spite of the person's being afraid, he took the action anyway. Therefore, a criterion for courage is action. That person's courage lies in the fact that he overcame his fears.

Another answer you might have given is, "When a person sets out to accomplish something in spite of enormous obstacles." Perhaps a person has a handicap, whether it be a physical handicap, an emotional handicap, or simply a severe lack of opportunity, and he or she overcomes it to become a successful scientist, entertainer or sports figure.

Franklin Delano Roosevelt became President of the United States in spite of being confined to a wheelchair due to polio.

Here again, the criterion for courage is not the handicap ...rather, it is the accomplishment due to the determination and persistence of the individual.

There's a flaw in our thinking if we perceive courage only in instances of extremes, and refuse to perceive it under our noses every day of our lives.

For courage is not found only in the very successful, or the very dedicated, or even the very strong. It is within each person. It is within you.

"I CAN"
Simply put, it is your inner sense of "I can."

Almost all of us have lost sight of the fact that it's natural for things to be easy. This is because we rarely experience our courageousness in a pure form. It's usually mixed with one or more of the other emotions, such as fear or anger or grief, and that dilutes its power. When that happens, we find it difficult to accomplish our objectives.

Begin now to perceive courageousness as a natural state, rather than as something unusual. You'll notice that you have a lot more energy to accomplish things, and there'll be less fighting with yourself and others.

You'll be on your way to being much more relaxed and at ease about everything you do. It will become easier to accomplish your goals and objectives — and you'll feel better, too.

Typical Courageousness Feelings
Alert, aware, alive, enthusiastic, persistent, supportive, energetic, vibrant, happy, cheerful, resilient.

Let's take a look at courageousness in terms of "I can," and then explore some of the ways we sabotage ourselves.

COURAGEOUSNESS WORKSHEET #1

Please check the items below which apply to you.

- ☐ I CAN drive in traffic.
- ☐ I CAN fry an egg.
- ☐ I CAN provide for my family.
- ☐ I CAN get up in the morning.
- ☐ I CAN ask for a raise.
- ☐ I CAN enjoy the sunset.
- ☐ I CAN give a gift.
- ☐ I CAN comfort the bereaved.
- ☐ I CAN offer guidance to my children.
- ☐ I CAN have a job.
- ☐ I CAN allow people their opinions.
- ☐ I CAN be silent.
- ☐ I CAN speak out.
- ☐ I CAN love.
- ☐ I CAN feel.
- ☐ I CAN be an individual.
- ☐ I CAN share my bounty.
- ☐ I CAN let go of my negativity.
- ☐ I CAN be happy.

Add some of your own here, too.

- ☐ I CAN _____
- ☐ I CAN _____
- ☐ I CAN _____
- ☐ I CAN _____
- ☐ I CAN _____
- ☐ I CAN _____
- ☐ I CAN _____

☐ I CAN _____

☐ I CAN _____

☐ I CAN _____

☐ I CAN _____

☐ I CAN _____

☐ I CAN _____

☐ I CAN _____

☐ I CAN _____

☐ I CAN _____

☐ I CAN _____

☐ I CAN _____

☐ I CAN _____

☐ I CAN _____

☐ I CAN _____

☐ I CAN _____

☐ I CAN _____

☐ I CAN _____

☐ I CAN _____

☐ I CAN _____

The list is endless, just as your courageousness is endless. There are no limits to it.

COURAGEOUSNESS WORKSHEET #2

However, we might not be *willing* to do all the things that are possible, so we tell ourselves that we *can't*. Check the items below which apply to you.

- ☐ I CAN'T drive in traffic; I might have an accident.
- ☐ I CAN'T fry an egg; it might burn.
- ☐ I CAN'T provide for my family; I'm not skilled enough.
- ☐ I CAN'T get up in the morning; I'm too tired.
- ☐ I CAN'T ask for a raise; my boss might fire me.
- ☐ I CAN'T enjoy the sunset; I haven't the time.
- ☐ I CAN'T give a gift; I don't know what they'd like.
- ☐ I CAN'T comfort the bereaved; it would only make them sadder to talk about it.
- ☐ I CAN'T offer guidance to my children; I'm too mixed up myself.
- ☐ I CAN'T have a job; I don't have the right connections.
- ☐ I CAN'T allow people their opinions; they might try to push them on me.
- ☐ I CAN'T be silent; I must express my feelings.
- ☐ I CAN'T speak out; people might get mad at me.
- ☐ I CAN'T love; I don't know how.
- ☐ I CAN'T feel; it's far too painful.
- ☐ I CAN'T be an individual; my parents wouldn't let me.
- ☐ I CAN'T share my bounty; there's only enough for me.
- ☐ I CAN'T achieve my goals; the world is too hard.
- ☐ I CAN'T let go of my negativity; what would be left?
- ☐ I CAN'T be happy; there's too much against me.

Now do some of your own.

- ☐ I CAN'T _____
- ☐ I CAN'T _____
- ☐ I CAN'T _____
- ☐ I CAN'T _____

☐ I CAN'T _____

☐ I CAN'T _____

☐ I CAN'T _____

☐ I CAN'T _____

☐ I CAN'T _____

☐ I CAN'T _____

☐ I CAN'T _____

☐ I CAN'T _____

☐ I CAN'T _____

☐ I CAN'T _____

☐ I CAN'T _____

☐ I CAN'T _____

☐ I CAN'T _____

☐ I CAN'T _____

☐ I CAN'T _____

☐ I CAN'T _____

☐ I CAN'T _____

☐ I CAN'T _____

☐ I CAN'T _____

As you've probably noticed, when we tell ourselves we can't, we usually also invent a reason to back us up, whether the reason is valid or not.

COURAGEOUSNESS WORKSHEET #3

There's something else which hampers our courageousness. I call it *unwillingness* or *"I won't."* It would look like this. Please check the items which apply to you.

- ☐ I WON'T drive in traffic; those creeps don't know how to drive.
- ☐ I WON'T fry an egg; make it yourself.
- ☐ I WON'T provide for my family; someone should provide for me.
- ☐ I WON'T get up in the morning; I don't feel like it.
- ☐ I WON'T ask for a raise; I'd rather complain.
- ☐ I WON'T take time to enjoy the sunset; I'd rather make them feel guilty about how hard I work.
- ☐ I WON'T give a gift; no one gives me anything.
- ☐ I WON'T comfort the bereaved; they might expect too much.
- ☐ I WON'T offer guidance to my children; let them figure it out for themselves the way I had to do.
- ☐ I WON'T have a job; why should they get off the hook?
- ☐ I WON'T allow people their opinions; who do they think they are?
- ☐ I WON'T be silent; everyone should listen to me.
- ☐ I WON'T speak out; let them stew in their own juice.
- ☐ I WON'T love; they'll only take advantage of me.
- ☐ I WON'T feel; they might think I'm weak.
- ☐ I WON'T be an individual; I'll make them suffer for what they did to me.
- ☐ I WON'T share my bounty; they'll only want more and more.
- ☐ I WON'T achieve my goals; what would I do to keep busy then?
- ☐ I WON'T let go of my negativity; how would I protect myself?
- ☐ I WON'T be happy; they might not feel guilty anymore.

Now it's time for you to add yours.

☐ I WON'T _____

☐ I WON'T _____

☐ I WON'T _____

☐ I WON'T _____

☐ I WON'T _____

☐ I WON'T _____

☐ I WON'T _____

☐ I WON'T _____

☐ I WON'T _____

☐ I WON'T _____

☐ I WON'T _____

☐ I WON'T _____

☐ I WON'T _____

☐ I WON'T _____

☐ I WON'T _____

☐ I WON'T _____

☐ I WON'T _____

☐ I WON'T _____

☐ I WON'T _____

☐ I WON'T _____

☐ I WON'T _____

☐ I WON'T _____

☐ I WON'T _____

☐ I WON'T _____

See, the *"I won't"* is usually accompanied by some hostile, unloving feeling. This always diminishes our natural *"I can"* abilities.

COURAGEOUSNESS WORKSHEET #4

Now I'd like you to make your own list. Fill in the right column first with things you think you cannot do. Then look over your list and discriminate. Put the word *can, can't* or *won't* in the second column, after the word "I."

If something is a *can't,* put down why you can't. If it's a *won't,* what's the reason? Why won't you? (You might want to refer to the *I won't* list on the previous page. Perhaps you'll find some of your own reasons there.)

You might also want to put down as many reasons for the *I can'ts* and the *I won'ts* as you can think of, because the first reasons you think of are not always the real reasons.

After you complete your list, you can review it every day for a while until you get *all* of your reasons written down. If you do this, I promise you some very interesting surprises as your subconscious computer begins to send up some of the old thoughts and feelings you've been unaware of.

I _____ _____

_____

I _____ _____

_____

I _____ _____

_____

I _____ _____

_____

I _____ _____

_____

I _____ _____

_____

I _____ _____
_____

I _____ _____
_____

I _____ _____
_____

I _____ _____
_____

I _____ _____
_____

I _____ _____
_____

I _____ _____
_____

I _____ _____
_____

I _____ _____
_____

I _____ _____
_____

I _____ _____
_____

Levels Of Courageousness

There are three levels of courageousness. These are determined by how much subconscious negativity and "I CAN'Ts" we hold as opposed to the amount of positive energy and "I CAN's" that we have made available to ourselves.

A scale of it might look like this:

	I CAN	I CAN'T
Top Band of Courageousness	75%	25%
Middle Band of Courageousness	50%	50%
Lower Band of Courageousness	25%	75%

As you can see, the middle of courageousness is 50% positive and 50% negative and this refers to programs you have stored on a subconscious level, as well as to your conscious thoughts. Therefore, you must attain that 50/50 balance on a subconscious, as well as conscious, level before you can start to *easily* maintain your positive energy. Once you achieve that, however, your progress can be very rapid because it becomes easy then to spot and eliminate the negatives the minute they arise.

One of the reasons for this is that your capacity to discriminate increases as you get rid of your negative feelings.

When you reach the top band of courageousness, you face life without fear, moving quickly, intuitively and appropriately. Then you can be a dynamic, charismatic person.

NOTES:

"I love you, world. You're so beautiful. I love the sky, and the sun, and the trees and flowers, and birds so lovely in the air, and animals with their families and their caringness, and the moon, and night with its secrets, and dawn with its promise, and noon with its light, and babies, and old people, and all the precious ones in between who struggle and love and strive for perfection. I love you, world. My love is boundless and pure and floods me with joy. I love you, love you, love you. And I love me."

A Person in Acceptance

CHAPTER 10

ACCEPTANCE

ACCEPTANCE: "To receive with approval or favor; to take or receive what is offered with a consenting mind; to consent or agree to; to understand."—*Webster.*

Acceptance is a very high energy state but the energy is light and inward, rather than being outwardly directed as it is in courageousness.

It is a condition of extreme well-being ranging from feelings of contentment to intense joy. We most commonly experience it as wholehearted love and understanding toward another person. We all experience it occasionally to some degree because it, like courageousness, is a state which is within each of us and is natural in us.

Acceptance means loving ourselves and others with all our vagaries and without being judgmental or critical. It is loving someone no matter how they are or what they do. It means loving the person, even if he or she does things we don't like or cannot approve of. It means discriminating and separating the beautiful essence of people from what their subconscious programs drive them to do, and loving that essence.

You might recognize the feeling by remembering a beautiful, perfect early spring day. Birds singing; trees beginning to bud; the air clear and warm and soft with the scent of spring. On such a day, you've probably felt within yourself the stirrings of a joy which usually lies dormant, buried beneath mountains of suppressed negative feelings. You feel good!

You might also recognize the feeling of acceptance as what you experience when you see a happy little baby or child. It's a happy, joyous feeling. You might smile at the baby, or talk to the child, with a friendliness and acceptance you wouldn't feel free to express with an adult.

Another example of the acceptance feeling is what you might call "being in love." Do you remember how you felt when you first fell in love with someone, before your AGFLAP feelings got stirred up and things went wrong? It's really a glorious feeling — light and warm and loving. Nothing bothers you when you feel that way. You can even laugh at all the petty annoyances that would usually bother you any other time.

And have you noticed how that feeling transforms people? Suddenly they're radiant and beautiful — skin glowing — eyes shining — they look years younger.

That joyous feeling, that deep inner state of beauty and love, is what we are calling acceptance. When we get rid of enough of our suppressed "I can'ts," we move naturally and easily into that state.

On the scale of *I can,* acceptance would be:

90% I CAN——10% I CAN'T

The acceptance worksheets which follow are to help you discriminate and to evaluate your relationships with loved ones, friends and others. The "Why?" column is particularly important, to help you see patterns in your thinking and in your emotions.

Once seen, you can evaluate these patterns and make decisions as to whether they are in the best interest of your happiness and peace of mind, and whether or not you wish to keep them.

Typical Acceptance Feelings

Loving, joyous, friendly, warm, glowing, beautiful, open, soft, gentle, tender, non-judgmental.

NOTES:

ACCEPTANCE WORKSHEET #1
Looking At Acceptance

Whom Do I Like
Or Love?

Why?

_____   _____

_____   _____

_____   _____

_____   _____

_____   _____

_____   _____

_____   _____

_____   _____

_____   _____

_____   _____

_____   _____

_____   _____

_____   _____

_____   _____

_____   _____

Whom Do I Like Or Love?	Why?

ACCEPTANCE WORKSHEET #2
Looking At Non-Acceptance

Whom Do I Not
Like Or Love?   Why?

_____   _____

_____   _____

_____   _____

_____   _____

_____   _____

_____   _____

_____   _____

_____   _____

_____   _____

_____   _____

_____   _____

_____   _____

_____   _____

Whom Do I Not
Like Or Love?   Why?

_____   _____
_____   _____
_____   _____
_____   _____
_____   _____
_____   _____
_____   _____
_____   _____
_____   _____
_____   _____
_____   _____
_____   _____
_____   _____
_____   _____
_____   _____
_____   _____
_____   _____
_____   _____
_____   _____

Quiet, still, calm, light, pure, perfect, flowing, glowing, boundless, timeless, ageless, still, whole, complete, aware, tranquil, serene, clear, centered, free, fulfilled, still, imperturbable.

A Person in Peace

CHAPTER 11

PEACE

PEACE: "An undisturbed state of mind; absence of mental conflict; serenity; calm; quiet; tranquility."—*Webster.*

Peace is at the very core of your being. You might catch an occasional fleeting glimpse of it at the seashore, or the mountains, or in meditation. This might mislead you into thinking that it's necessary to withdraw from the world in order to find peace.

The fact is that the peace you find in such retreats is only a temporary escape from the everyday problems which stir up your suppressed negative feelings, your AGFLAP. You might go to a mountaintop, feel very peaceful after being there for a while, but within a short time after you return home, you can be just as caught up in the emotions as before you left. In fact, you might even feel your AGFLAP emotions more acutely, in contrast to the quiet experience you had in the mountains.

There's more to peace than just running away from the things that disturb you. It's necessary to get rid of the AGFLAP, so that you can be a happy, productive person no matter where you are or what your role in life may be.

If you cannot feel inwardly peaceful in the midst of the world and your daily activities, it's an indication that you still have subconscious negative feelings and you'll never be completely satisfied until they are gone. This is because, as long as you have those suppressed feelings, you'll be out of touch with your "I" sense and unable to sustain the happiness and peace of mind you crave.

Every unhappiness you experience is your "I" sense being disturbed and obscured by the negative feelings, your AGFLAP.

This being so, then everything you do is an attempt to regain your "I" sense, to get back to that joy and peacefulness which has been disturbed by the negative feelings. All your actions are merely attempts to regain that happiness and peace of mind which is your basic nature.

And when you succeed in quieting the inner disturbances, you get in touch with yourself, your "I" sense, and you feel happy.

The objective in getting rid of your suppressed feelings is to achieve that state of peace which will allow you to be aware of your inner center of quietude, even as you go about your daily tasks.

Another point I'd like to make about the state of peace is that, in terms of energy, it is all energy, instantly available, but at rest. You might compare it to the ocean. Quiet, still and deep, yet with tremendous energy contained in the force of the water when it's directed and focused.

What this means in terms of your ability to function is that you are not disturbed and thrown off course by things that happen in your world. You feel competent to deal with anything that comes up.

If necessary, you can communicate with others in any emotional voice which may be necessary to get through to them. If they're in anger and shouting, they might not be able to hear you if you speak softly. Therefore, you might have to raise your voice in order to communicate with those people. It may be almost impossible to imagine it, but you could even be shouting at someone and still maintain your inner state of quietness if you have no suppressed negative feelings remaining.

Without your AGFLAP to bother you, you can function at the highest level of efficiency. Think about how you feel at those times when nothing is happening to stir you up and when you're focused on something you like to do. If you're a musician, this might happen when you're practicing or playing for your own pleasure. If you're a mechanic, you might notice it when you're working on your car. If you like to do woodworking, or paint pictures, or fish, or listen to music, or just relax on your porch, there's a wonderful feeling of being quiet inside when your mind is concentrated and quiet. That's peace. You can notice it at times when your mind is concentrated if you know what to look for. But it's so natural that we don't really notice it much. We only notice its *absence* when something happens to stir up the AGFLAP.

Peace Is You Being Quiet Inside

So why not start to notice it when it happens? And recognize it for what it is — you being you. And you may find that the quietest times are really the happiest times, and that might encourage you to make it permanent.

And when you are totally free of the suppressed feelings, you are imperturbable. Then no one and no thing can disturb you.

Peace is 100% I CAN.

PEACE WORKSHEET

Write down the things you do that make you feel peaceful. This is a nice way of reminding yourself that you can be peaceful sometimes, even if it isn't all the time. It can also get you looking at the *feeling* of peacefulness, and recognizing just what it feels like. Most of the time, we're so plagued by the *absence* of peace, by the noise of the emotions, that we don't know a peaceful feeling when we have one.

This is a little like wearing shoes. If your shoes fit well, and they support your feet, and they're comfortable, you can walk for miles and miles and never think about having shoes on. But just put on a pair that are too tight and watch what happens. You can barely walk across the room without pain. You surely do know that you have shoes on — and can hardly wait to get them off. This is what the negative emotions feel like. They pinch, they hurt, and we certainly know we have them.

But the feeling of peace is different. It's so natural and comfortable, and it fits us so well, that we rarely notice when we're in it. So it will help a lot if you'll just quietly start to notice when you're peaceful. You'll begin to see how nice it is, and it will remind you of your true nature which is always there, at the center of your being.

Things I Do Which Make Me Feel Peaceful

_____

_____

_____

_____

_____

Things I Do Which Make Me Feel Peaceful

Energy Summary Of The Positive Emotional States
(A further breakdown of the Energy Level Chart)

	I CAN	I CANNOT
COURAGEOUSNESS is the most	25%	75%
energetic in terms of outward		
action. When we are in courageous-	50%	50%
ness, we can and do take immediate,		
intuitive, appropriate action. In	75%	25%
fact, the action is often completed		
before our slow thinking process		
can begin to figure it out.		
ACCEPTANCE is even more	85%	15%
energetic but it is mostly inner		
energy. Objectives are very easy to	90%	10%
achieve without the necessity of a		
lot of outward action. The way to	95%	5%
resolve situations comes to us		
intuitively, with ease, and then any		
necessary follow-through is done		
without effort.		
PEACE is all energy instantly	100%	0%
available...but at rest. It is an		
extremely quiet, most effective and		
efficient state.		

NOTES

CHAPTER 12

FIND YOUR HOME BASE

What do I mean by the term "home base?"

I use this term to describe a person's general or overall energy level. It's the energy level the person is in most of the time and to which he or she returns. Even though it might be a painful emotional state, in an odd way the person feels comfortable there. It's like an old shoe. If you've ever gone somewhere, perhaps to a party or to a new job, where you felt extremely uncomfortable and couldn't wait to leave, your discomfort was probably due to the fact that the people there were in a different energy level or home base than yours. You might even have said to a friend afterwards, "They were not my kind of people."

Let me give you some examples of the various home bases.

We all know those people who live with a gray cloud over their heads. We see them walking around in a continual state of depression and no one can ever seem to lift them out of it. Nothing ever seems to work for them. They simply cannot win, no matter what they do, so they give up after a while and stop trying. Their home base is apathy.

Those with their home base in grief are in a slightly higher energy level. They haven't given up yet so they may keep trying and failing. Their overall feeling is, "Nobody loves me; nobody understands me," and they keep looking for that person who will finally understand and make it right. Unfortunately, even when they find someone, they often drive the person away with their sadness and negative attitude. Their favorite expression might even be "good grief."

People whose home base is fear are always worried about something. In extreme cases, they'll worry about everything. They'll worry about what to say, how to act, and what others might be thinking about them. Of course, they will sometimes move up into the energy levels of lust or anger, or down into the grief and apathy energy levels, but they'll always tend to settle back into the range of emotions characterized by fear. They're usually nervous individuals and have trouble making decisions or taking action. They will definitely resist taking any action which might, even remotely, carry a risk with it.

There is a great deal of confusion about the subject of lust. It is commonly thought of as relating only to sex. However it is not exclusively sexual. Lust as truly defined is a hunger or wanting or thirsting for something. People in a lust home base are usually wanting something all the time. They are driven by their subconscious programs. They tend to *use* people with no regard for the other person's feelings or well-being. They'll strive for positions of power so they can exert the control they crave over others. They're often obsessed with sex or possessions or power and they'll do anything to get what they want. Unfortunately, any satisfaction they may derive from actually getting what they want is momentary. Once the object is obtained, it is usually soon discarded. Even though they may *outwardly* seem to have everything they want and to be successful, they're not really happy because they're always wanting the next thing which they haven't got. This is a very frustrating way to live.

People whose home base is in anger are easily aroused. Sometimes the least little thing will set off an explosion. They're sometimes described by others as "having a short fuse." They are often crabby, ill-tempered, and don't have the time or inclination to listen to anyone. They feel that there is only one point of view (theirs) to be considered in any discussion. They scream and shout and you might walk away from a meeting with them feeling as though you'd been run over by a steam roller.

Those people with their home base in pride don't listen to others either, but their attitude is of a more cool, detached, and disdainful attitude that can make you feel as though you are incapable and don't really matter. They'll have you believe that they know everything and that you have nothing to contribute. You might develop an inferiority complex around such people and try very hard to get them to like you or approve of you. This rarely works, however. Because of their subconscious insecurity, they try to be secure by making others feel insecure. This is the only way they can feel safe.

Another type of person whose energy level is in pride is the one who boasts about him or herself all the time. He might be a cocky, swaggering show-off who openly puts others down. He can be very hard to take because no matter what happens, even when he's wrong, he's always right, and he's sure to let you know it.

A person's home base is the energy level at which that person feels most comfortable, and to which he or she always comes back. Someone in the energy level of grief might take charge of the softball team, but when things go wrong that person would quickly go back to his home base of grief. Someone in fear might courageously take a chance on something but when it becomes too threatening, he or she would back off and allow the fear to stop them. Someone in courageousness might become afraid or sad about something that's happened, but he wouldn't stay there long. He'd quickly move back to his home base of courageousness because that's the energy level in which he feels most comfortable.

To start getting the idea, you might first decide on the home bases of characters on television or in cartoons. They're often broadly drawn and easy to spot. This would be an interesting activity to do with a friend because it's lots of fun and you can share ideas and both learn from it.

Next, you might try determining the home bases of people you know. Remember that with a real person, it can be more difficult because appearances are not always what they seem. True feelings can be hidden and the signs might be very subtle. Still, doing this can give you a better feel of home bases.

Then you can go on to determine your own home base. Be sure to relax when you do this and allow yourself to feel your way through. There is no right or wrong way. It's not a test or an absolute scale. It's just an opportunity for you to look at yourself in a different way. You might even decide that you have a dual home base, that there is more than one emotional state which you experience often or feel comfortable with. That's all right too.

It's very important to remember that no matter where your home base is, you always have courageousness as part of you. It's always there, no matter where you are on the energy scale most of the time. If it weren't for that fact, we would be stuck forever in our AGFLAP.

Another important point to remember is that you can change your home base. Sometimes people accomplish that by making a strong decision to change. Sometimes they do it by getting rid of their AGFLAP. A lot of people use the Release$_{sm}$ technique to do this. This is the method taught in the Sedona Institute classes.

Some attitudes and behavior follow which are representative of each emotional state or energy level. You can use these lists to help you determine your emotional home base and that of others. After you've decided where you fit, you might want to ask a friend where they think your home base is. This would give you an idea of how others perceive you and help you gain even more insights into yourself.

Please go to each one and mark those attitudes and behavior that apply to you. You can use the following letters if you like.

O = Often
S = Sometimes
R = Rarely
N = Never

You may wish to eliminate the last category, the "Never" one, and simply leave those spaces blank. I suggest that you make your marks in pencil, because as you begin to discriminate more clearly about emotions, your attitudes and behavior may change and you could then change the entry. For example, your "O" may become an "S" after a while, and then a bit later may even become an "R" or an "N." It will be satisfying and encouraging for you to make the changes in your book.

The blank lines at the end of each emotion are for you to write in your own attitudes and behavior which are not already included in the list. In fact, that could be the most helpful part of the whole exercise, because this book is really about you. The things we've included here are just some ideas to get you started on the exciting journey of learning about yourself.

So take your time, allow your discrimination to open, encourage your "I" sense to take charge, and watch your life change. Have fun!

APATHY

Apathy Attitudes

— What's the use?
— Why bother?
— Who cares?
— Nobody cares.
— I don't care.
— That's life.
— I'm so confused.
— It just wasn't meant to be.
— I can't cope.
— Leave me alone.
— I just can't keep up.
— It's too much for me.
— They wouldn't want me anyway.
— I'm just no good at that.
— I'm worthless.
— I have no talent for it.
— Nobody wants me.
— It's not my job.
— I'm bored.
— There's nothing I can do.
— It's my karma.
— Nothing matters.
— Feeling ugly.
— There's nobody to talk to.
— I'm too old.
— There's nothing to do.
— There are no jobs anyway.
— I'm resigned to my fate.
— It's too late.
— I'm disillusioned.

— _____
— _____
— _____
— _____

Apathetic Behavior

— Sleeping a lot
— Watching TV too much
— Lying around the house
— Avoiding people
— Behaving repetitively
— Sighing
— Waiting for others to do it
— Behaving mechanically
— Dressing sloppily
— Tuning out
— Procrastinating
— Making excuses
— Blaming others for your own failures
— Spacing out
— Daydreaming excessively
— Not dealing with reality
— Drinking too much
— Taking drugs
— Giving up
— Working too little
— Being very unproductive
— Being dependent
— Being listless
— "Cursing the darkness..."
— Being inattentive
— Being humorless
— Being forgetful
— Being indecisive

— _____
— _____
— _____
— _____

Apathy Attitudes   Apathetic Behavior

— _____   — _____

— _____   — _____

— _____   — _____

— _____   — _____

— _____   — _____

— _____   — _____

— _____   — _____

— _____   — _____

— _____   — _____

— _____   — _____

— _____   — _____

— _____   — _____

— _____   — _____

— _____   — _____

— _____   — _____

— _____   — _____

GRIEF

Grief Attitudes

— I can't stand it any more.
— Please put me out of my misery.
— It hurts too much.
— No one understands me.
— I wish I were dead.
— Woe is me.
— If only I had another chance.
— I'm so sorry.
— Please forgive me.
— I couldn't help it.
— I feel guilty enough already.
— It's not my fault.
— Won't someone please help me?
— Don't you love me anymore?
— I'm no good.
— I deserve to be punished.
— I can't live without you.
— My life is over.
— Why me?
— I'm so lonely.
— I wish I had someone to love me.
— I'm a walking wound.
— Please don't leave me.
— What will I do?
— How can I live?
— Nobody loves me.

— _____
— _____
— _____
— _____

Grief Behavior

— Crying
— Sighing
— Sobbing
— Moping
— Sleeping very poorly
— Withdrawing
— Eating too much
— Losing appetite
— Whining
— Clinging
— Pleading
— Begging
— Holding on
— Being dependent
— Making excuses
— Clamming up
— Dressing sloppily
— Getting sick

— _____
— _____
— _____
— _____
— _____
— _____
— _____
— _____

116

Grief Attitudes

— _____

— _____

— _____

— _____

— _____

— _____

— _____

— _____

— _____

— _____

— _____

— _____

— _____

— _____

— _____

— _____

— _____

— _____

Grief Behavior

— _____

— _____

— _____

— _____

— _____

— _____

— _____

— _____

— _____

— _____

— _____

— _____

— _____

— _____

— _____

— _____

— _____

— _____

FEAR

Fear Attitudes

— Stay away from me!
— Let's stop now.
— What was that???
— Caution
— Look out!!!
— Let me out of here!
— Help!
— Who's there???
— Wariness
— Afraid to change
— What if I get caught?
— Let's stop while we're ahead.
— Anxiety
— Apprehensiveness
— You can't trust anyone!
— They're all crooks at heart.
— What's your angle?
— What's in it for you?
— You always have to be on guard.
— Shyness
— You won't catch me taking chances.
— Don't move!!!
— They're watching.
— Quiet! They'll hear.
— Better safe than sorry.
— They're all out to get you.
— The game's rigged.
— What's the catch?
— Trapped feeling
— Vulnerability
— Mistrust

— _____

— _____

— _____

Fear Behavior

— Looking over your shoulder
— Running away
— Hiding
— Changing locks
— Playing it safe
— Screaming
— Keeping quiet
— Freezing
— Making excuses
— Lying
— Whistling in the dark
— Lying low
— Fidgeting
— Trying to be invisible
— Clamming up
— Letting someone else go first
— Being a wallflower
— Being cynical
— Avoiding change
— Staying in a rut
— Being unwilling to speak up
— Lacking assertiveness
— Bragging to cover up insecurity
— Blaming others
— Not making decisions
— Not speaking your own mind
— Sneaking around
— Being covert
— Being underhanded
— Hanging on to outmoded ideas

— _____

— _____

— _____

Fear Attitudes

— _____

— _____

— _____

— _____

— _____

— _____

— _____

— _____

— _____

— _____

— _____

— _____

— _____

— _____

— _____

— _____

— _____

— _____

— _____

— _____

— _____

Fear Behavior

— _____

— _____

— _____

— _____

— _____

— _____

— _____

— _____

— _____

— _____

— _____

— _____

— _____

— _____

— _____

— _____

— _____

— _____

— _____

— _____

LUST

Lust Attitudes

— I want it all.
— I want it now.
— I want more.
— It's never enough.
— Gimme, gimme, gimme!
— Let's do it again.
— I don't have enough to share.
— Give me some of yours.
— Why should you have any?
— I'll never stop!
— I'm never satisfied.
— More, more, more.
— Once is never enough.
— I have to have it.
— It's mine, all mine!
— I'll eat mine and yours too.
— I don't care what they think.
— Faster, let's go faster.
— I can't stay away.
— Please give it all to me.
— Give me bigger portions.
— I've just got to do it again.
— I'll cheat if I must but I've got to have it.
— **I don't care.** I'll do it anyway.
— If they don't like it, tough!

— _____
— _____
— _____
— _____
— _____

Lust Behavior

— Pushiness
— Possessiveness
— Compulsion
— Addiction
— Desperation
— Grabbing things
— Recklessness
— Selfishness
— Miserliness
— Greediness
— Self absorption
— Overeating
— Envy
— Cheating of people to get what one wants
— Cheating on mate
— Theft to buy drugs
— Robbery of liquor stores
— Forfeit of long-range benefits for instant gratification
— Constant search for gratification
— Step on people
— Use of people
— Destruction of people to get ahead
— Disregard of moral values
— Covert undermining
— Blind ambition

— _____
— _____
— _____
— _____

120

Lust Attitudes

— _____

— _____

— _____

— _____

— _____

— _____

— _____

— _____

— _____

— _____

— _____

— _____

— _____

— _____

— _____

— _____

— _____

— _____

— _____

Lust Behavior

— _____

— _____

— _____

— _____

— _____

— _____

— _____

— _____

— _____

— _____

— _____

— _____

— _____

— _____

— _____

— _____

— _____

— _____

ANGER

Anger Attitudes

— Hateful
— Sarcastic
— Drop dead.
— Got to get revenge at any cost.
— Don't you dare!
— I'll make you sorry.
— You'll wish you'd never been born.
— Stay away from me or else!
— Don't you *ever* try that again.
— If I ever get my hands on you...
— You're done for!
— You'd better watch out!
— I'll break your head.
— I'll knock you silly.
— Murderous
— Stay away from me ...I'm dangerous!
— Chip on the shoulder.
— Touchy
— Crabby
— Hot under the collar
— A short fuse
— Hot-tempered
— Violent
— Unpredictable
— Threatening
— Abrasive
— Nasty

— _____
— _____
— _____
— _____

Anger Behavior

— Attacking
— Gossiping viciously
— Hitting
— Kicking
— Shouting
— Blaming
— Violence
— Criticizing destructively
— Biting
— Throwing things
— Destroying property
— Hurting people
— Driving recklessly
— Picking fights
— Being moody
— Sulking
— Simmering
— Seething quietly
— Undermining people
— Stepping on people
— Abusing people
— Hurting yourself
— Having fits of pique
— Indulging in temper tantrums
— Having fits of rage
— Taking it out on animals
— Taking it out on inanimate objects

— _____
— _____
— _____
— _____

Anger Attitudes

— _____

— _____

— _____

— _____

— _____

— _____

— _____

— _____

— _____

— _____

— _____

— _____

— _____

— _____

— _____

— _____

— _____

— _____

Anger Behavior

— _____

— _____

— _____

— _____

— _____

— _____

— _____

— _____

— _____

— _____

— _____

— _____

— _____

— _____

— _____

— _____

— _____

— _____

PRIDE

Pride Attitudes

— Look at what *I* did.
— *I'd* never do that sort of thing.
— I'm better than that.
— I always know best.
— I'm above all that.
— I'm just too good.
— Oh! you poor thing.
— You're just not up to it.
— Perhaps someday you'll understand.
— Some people just don't know any better.
— You're not ready for that yet.
— You're just not advanced enough.
— Presumptuous
— Condescending
— Superior
— Doesn't everyone?
— Do you know who I am?
— I'd never have those problems.
— It's in the breeding.
— They'll never make it.
— They've no imagination.
— You don't know who you're dealing with.
— Do you know who my friends are?
— I know your boss.
— Above it all
— Unwilling to learn

— _____
— _____
— _____

Pride Behavior

— Looking down one's nose at others
— Disregarding others
— Criticizing
— Putting others down
— Ignoring people
— Staying with cliques
— Being closed minded
— Disregarding input from others
— Laughing at others' efforts
— Making snide remarks
— Raising your eyebrows
— Being pushy
— Making jokes about people
— Being catty
— Trying to hold others back
— Strutting
— Talking down to people
— Giving unasked-for advice
— Showing off
— Using things as status symbols
— Name-dropping
— Observing rather than participating
— Comparing oneself and others
— Holding on to prejudices
— Ignoring others
— Judging others
— Being IN

— _____
— _____
— _____

124

Pride Attitudes

— _____

— _____

— _____

— _____

— _____

— _____

— _____

— _____

— _____

— _____

— _____

— _____

— _____

— _____

— _____

— _____

— _____

— _____

Pride Behavior

— _____

— _____

— _____

— _____

— _____

— _____

— _____

— _____

— _____

— _____

— _____

— _____

— _____

— _____

— _____

— _____

— _____

COURAGEOUSNESS

Courageous Attitudes

- __ I can.
- __ You can.
- __ Everyone can.
- __ Resourceful
- __ Recognizes people's potential
- __ Feels people are basically good
- __ It's easy to get ahead.
- __ You can do it.
- __ If i can do it, anyone can.
- __ Independent
- __ I don't dwell on the problem...
  I look for the solution.
- __ Cheerful attitude
- __ Ability to concentrate
- __ Purposeful
- __ Enthusiasm for work
- __ Enthusiastic about life
- __ Supportive of others
- __ Adventurous
- __ Spontaneous
- __ Quick to learn
- __ Open-minded
- __ Flexible...willing to bend
- __ Open to hearing others'
  opinions
- __ Willing to make decisions
- __ Willing to take responsibility
- __ Perceptive
- __ Often operates intuitively
- __ High sense of integrity
- __ Honorable
- __ Good moral character
- __ High energy
- __ Clarity of mind
- __ Resilient
- __ Zest for life
- __ Generally has many friends
- __ Dynamic

Courageous Behavior

- __ Needing little sleep
- __ Often working long hours
- __ Enjoying life
- __ Being faithful
- __ Making decisions quickly
- __ Following through with
  needed action
- __ Achieving personal goals
- __ Self-starting
- __ Often being in charge
- __ Being looked up to generally
- __ Comforting friends in trouble
- __ Listening well
- __ Giving credit to others
- __ Delegating successfully
- __ Being competitive
- __ Usually wins
- __ Undertaking entrepreneurial
  activities
- __ Succeeding at many things
- __ Not fearing failure
- __ Willing to try again
- __ Bolstering others
- __ Source of encouragement
- __ Source of strength
- __ Not making excuses
- __ Not blaming others
- __ Speaking forthrightly
- __ Considering others
- __ Accepting others' ideas
- __ Encouraging others
- __ Making strong
  commitment to ideals
- __ Daring to take risks
- __ _____
- __ _____

126

Courageous Attitudes

— ————————————————

— ———————————————— .

— ————————————————

— ————————————————

— ————————————————

— ————————————————

— ————————————————

— ————————————————

— ————————————————

— ————————————————

— ————————————————

— ————————————————

— ————————————————

— ————————————————

— ————————————————

— ————————————————

— ————————————————

— ————————————————

Courageous Behavior

— ————————————————

— ————————————————

— ————————————————

— ————————————————

— ————————————————

— ————————————————

— ————————————————

— ————————————————

— ————————————————

— ————————————————

— ————————————————

— ————————————————

— ————————————————

— ————————————————

— ————————————————

— ————————————————

— ————————————————

— ————————————————

ACCEPTANCE

Acceptance Attitudes

— Loving
— Joyful
— In tune with life
— Feeling of well-being
— I'm okay.
— You're okay.
— Sense of belonging
— Understanding
— Light, high energy
— Fullness of loving
— Considerate of each being
— Gentle
— Delighted with life
— Inner tickle
— Wonder at the beauty of life
— Embracing life
— Feeling beautiful
— Feeling good toward others
— Appreciation of others as they are
— Sense of humor
— Feeling balanced
— Tenderness
— Appreciation of yourself
— Playful
— Enjoyment of life
— Openness
— Friendly
— Graciousness
— Insightful
— Compassionate
— Feeling of abundance
— Non-judgmental
— Cheerful
— Giving
— Happy alone

Acceptance Behavior

— Generous to others
— Having commitment to ideals
— Having childlike qualities
— Laughing easily
— Encouraging others
— Enjoying others' success
— Enjoying the game more than the winning
— Taking happiness from within
— Having the ability to enjoy being alone
— Enjoying spending quiet time
— Seeing the good in people
— Having deep sense of integrity
— Not needing to change things
— Accepting of others
— Considerate toward ALL beings
— Living in harmony with nature
— Defusing disturbances in others
— Easy going
— Not needing things
— Appreciating beauty
— Taking time to smell the flowers
— Working easily
— Staying calm under pressure
— Exhibiting high level of self-awareness
— Open to growth and movement
— Uplifting to be with
— Taking time to listen
— Nice to be around
— Smiling
— Loving people
— Giving

Acceptance Attitudes

— _____

— _____

— _____

— _____

— _____

— _____

— _____

— _____

— _____

— _____

— _____

— _____

— _____

— _____

— _____

— _____

— _____

— _____

Acceptance Behavior

— _____

— _____

— _____

— _____

— _____

— _____

— _____

— _____

— _____

— _____

— _____

— _____

— _____

— _____

— _____

— _____

— _____

— _____

PEACE

Peaceful Attitudes

___ Serene
___ Calm
___ Quietness
___ High state of awareness
___ Sense of perfection in all things
___ Stillness
___ Feeling of freedom
___ Imperturbable
___ Sense of all power available but at rest
___ No need to demonstrate abilities
___ Feeling of Oneness
___ Fully open discrimination
___ Feeling light
___ Tranquility
___ Complete unto yourself
___ Sense of flowing with things
___ Feeling of inner space
___ Boundlessness
___ Agelessness
___ Total fulfillment
___ Inner youthfulness

___ _____
___ _____
___ _____
___ _____
___ _____
___ _____
___ _____

Peaceful Behavior

___ Quiet demeanor
___ Endless patience
___ Putting others before self
___ Knowing
___ Having strength of convictions
___ Totally unselfish
___ Not needing to convince others
___ Letting others have their way...with love
___ Having quietly twinkling eyes
___ Showing kindness to all
___ Letting others find their own strength
___ Letting others learn through their own experience
___ Dedicating oneself single-mindedly to helping others
___ Having no selfish motives
___ Refraining from telling others what to do
___ Allowing others to find their own way
___ Seeing the Oneness in each atom
___ Calming others by being present
___ Offering loving guidance for the other one to take or not
___ Being free to do or not to do anything and everything

___ _____
___ _____
___ _____

Peaceful Attitudes

— ———————————
— ———————————
— ———————————
— ———————————
— ———————————
— ———————————
— ———————————
— ———————————
— ———————————
— ———————————
— ———————————
— ———————————
— ———————————
— ———————————
— ———————————
— ———————————
— ———————————
— ———————————

Peaceful Behavior

— ———————————
— ———————————
— ———————————
— ———————————
— ———————————
— ———————————
— ———————————
— ———————————
— ———————————
— ———————————
— ———————————
— ———————————
— ———————————
— ———————————
— ———————————
— ———————————
— ———————————
— ———————————

CHAPTER 13

FOR THE LOVE OF AGFLAP

Let's look at what you sacrifice in order to preserve, protect and maintain your AGFLAP.

You Sacrifice Energy. As you've seen, your energy is drained by the feelings. Even when you're in one of the higher energy emotions such as anger, you may still feel exhausted when the attack passes. And guilty. And remorseful. And out of control. And frightened by the power of the emotion.

You Sacrifice Clarity. When the feelings are aroused, you can't think clearly. You're unable to see all your available options and you end up making decisions that are not in your own best interest.

You Sacrifice Productivity. In trying to escape the feelings, people often turn to drugs, alcohol, too much sleep, and other destructive behavior. This affects the productivity of the individual. Many corporate problems are created by absenteeism and emotional burnout caused by the pressure cooker of feelings.

You Sacrifice Your Personal Power. By allowing the feelings to control you and your behavior, you are assigning your power to the feelings. And since the feelings are based on information received and decisions made long ago, many of them when you were a child, your behavior will often reflect a childish point of view if it's motivated by feelings.

You Sacrifice Your "I Can." Just as feelings are related to levels of energy, they also reflect levels of "I can" and "I can't." The AGFLAP feelings are varying degrees of "I can't." Courageousness, acceptance and peace are degrees of "I can." Apathy is the greatest degree of "I can't."

You Sacrifice Love. It's impossible to talk about feelings without saying something about them as non-love. Just as the AGFLAP feelings represent varying degrees of the lack of energy and "I can't," they also reflect levels of non-love, or the lack of lovingness. Most people don't realize that their deep inner nature is that of loving. This is because it's been so obscured for so long by the AGFLAP, that they now feel they must use the AGFLAP to try to regain the love. We'll cry for love — we'll beg for love — we'll scream and shout for love — we'll tremble for love — we'll even kill for love. And it doesn't work. So we become more and more unhappy, unloved and unloving.

The reason it doesn't work is that you cannot obtain love from outside yourself. It is not there. It's within you that all the love exists and when you feel love, it's the love feelings within yourself that you feel. Think about it. Ask yourself where the feeling is when you feel it.

The funny thing is that we're always being told that we should be more loving. And we try and try to be more loving. "Love thy neighbor," for example. Many people try very hard to live up to those principles we were taught as children. So what gets in the way? Why don't we have a beautiful, loving world if we all have lovingness as our basic nature?

I believe that it's non-love that interferes. I believe that it's our accumulated AGFLAP that stops us and that we'll never be truly happy until we get rid of it.

And look at how our values become distorted by feelings. We lose sight of the beauty of a person when we're angry with that person. And we become blinded to the fact that a person is more important than a feeling. Then we add fuel to the fire by justifying, and blaming, and threatening, and sometimes by violence. When all we were trying to do, really, was to make that person do whatever we thought we needed them to do so that we could love them. Now, wouldn't it be better to eliminate the anger, and simply love the person the way he or she is? I think so.

Something we tend to forget is that we have the ability to love another person, even if that person doesn't do everything our way. Try it and see.

Ask yourself, "Could I love this person anyway, even if he or she does such and such?"

Another good question is, "How would I feel if I wanted this person to do what he or she is doing?"

So the next time you're not feeling loving toward someone close to you, try these questions. You'll be pleasantly surprised.

CHAPTER 14

AFTERWORD

Congratulations! By reading this book, you've started on a path of self-awareness and positive change that will get better as time goes by if you stick with it. Just by reading about emotions, you'll have gained a deeper awareness of your own emotional nature. You might also be noticing more often when a feeling is stirred up and the effect that that feeling has on your thinking.

But becoming aware is only the first step to mastering your emotions. It's also important to take action. Try some of the suggestions for getting yourself out of destructive and uncomfortable feelings when you notice that they are stirred up. If you do, you'll begin to see which particular approaches work best for you.

And when you are able to master your emotions, you'll notice that your thinking begins to change also. You'll naturally begin to think positively and constructively when the negative and destructive feelings are out of the way.

You might want to read again the sections of the book which seem to apply to yourself. I think that each time you read them, your discrimination will be opened a bit more and you'll see something helpful that you missed before.

At times when you notice that you're experiencing a particular emotion, read the section that relates to that emotion and try one of the "remedies." That's the kind of ongoing dedication to your personal growth that will make quite a difference as time goes by.

Mastering your emotions will bring about an increased self-confidence that will allow you to enjoy your life and to appreciate yourself and other people much more. It's so important to your sense of well-being to know that you don't have to be the victim of your emotions any longer. Many people have already discovered that. You can, too. Good luck and my very best wishes to you.

GLOSSARY OF TERMS

AGFLAP Apathy, grief, fear, lust, anger, pride. All the feelings which bother you.

CAP Courageousness, Acceptance, Peace. You, minus your AGFLAP; a state of happiness.

CONSCIOUS MIND The part of your mind that you're aware of; i.e., the thoughts you're thinking now.

DISCRIMINATION This is your ability to see things correctly, as they are. It also means your ability to tell one thing from another.

DISCRIMINATOR This relates to discrimination. It is the part of your mind which is like a camera lens. In a camera, the lens opens or closes according to the degree of light needed to take the picture. In your mind, the discriminator opens or closes according to the degree of emotion stirred up. When your discriminator is closed, your "I" sense loses control, and the programs take over and direct your actions and behavior.

ESCAPE	Trying to get away from the uncomfortable thoughts and feelings. We try to relieve the discomfort by looking away from them and putting our attention on something else such as TV, movies, vacations, etc. Another way we might try to escape feelings is by deadening ourselves so that we can't feel them anymore. We might use drugs and/or alcohol for this.
FEELING	The device our programs use to control us.
HOME BASE	The general or overall energy level of a person. It is the feeling level where the person feels most comfortable, and to which he or she always returns.
"I" SENSE	This is your sense of who you are, your identity. It's the part of you that is positive, clear, loving, powerful and smart. Your "I" sense becomes obscured and covered over as you accumulate the negative AGFLAP emotions. Your "I" sense always knows the best thing to do, but often cannot be heard because the AGFLAP takes over and pushes you into unwise actions.
PROGRAMS	These are things that you were told and decisions you made in the past about the way the world is and how you should behave in it.

The programs are stored in the sub-conscious part of your mind. When a past program is activated by something that happens to you, it stirs up your feelings, which causes your discriminator to close. This overrides your "I" sense; then the old program controls your behavior.

SENSES

Your five senses: taste, touch, hearing, smell, sight. Also includes your emotional feeling sense.

SUBCONSCIOUS MIND

The part of your mind that you're unaware of, the automatic pilot. This is the computer section and includes recording and replaying functions.

SUPPRESS

Pushing thoughts and feelings into the subconscious. When our feelings become uncomfortable, we try to suppress them, to make ourselves unaware of them so we don't have to experience them.

About Sedona Institute Seminars

If you found the information and suggestions in this book helpful, you may wish to go further and learn the Release℠ technique taught only in Sedona Institute seminars around the country.

SEDONA INSTITUTE BASIC COURSE—In these group classes, you're able to explore the whole range of feelings and emotions in a much more personal way. You can ask questions and be gently guided through the experience of letting go of troublesome emotions. Once you've completed this two-weekend course, you have a personal tool you can use from then on to continue your growth in the fastest way possible. Two weekends —consecutive Saturdays and Sundays—10 to 5:30. Presented in many cities around the country.

SEDONA INSTITUTE RESISTANCE COURSE—This four-session series focuses on how to eliminate inner resistances that interfere with goal achievement and your efficient functioning in work and home situations. For graduates of the Sedona Institute Basic Course only.

SEDONA INSTITUTE PROGRAMS COURSE—This three-day course explores the programs you've accumulated and shows you how to work directly on the program which is currently operative in your life. A lot of personal work is done with each participant in this group workshop. For graduates of the Sedona Institute Basic and Resistance Courses only.

SEDONA INSTITUTE 6-DAY INTENSIVE—This seminar is conducted only twice a year in beautiful Sedona, Arizona. Participants explore their programs in an unusual and experiential way. For graduates of the Sedona Institute Basic and Resistance Courses only.

SEDONA INSTITUTE 9-DAY ADVANCED INTENSIVE—Held only once or twice a year in Sedona, Arizona, this seminar is structured to provide a personal and in-depth exploration of the truth behind your programs. Only for graduates of all the above Sedona Institute Courses.

If you are interested in receiving more information about the Sedona Institute and a schedule of upcoming classes, as well as a catalog of other books and tapes available from Freedom Publications, please write or call:

SEDONA INSTITUTE
2408 Arizona Biltmore Circle
Suite #115
Phoenix, AZ 85016
Telephone: (602) 956-8766